The People Pleaser's Guide to

Putting Yourself First

Your step-by-step handbook to self-care and
living in alignment with your values

HOLLIE AZZOPARDI

affirm
press

First published by Affirm Press in 2022
Boon Wurrung Country
28 Thistlethwaite Street
South Melbourne VIC 3205
affirmpress.com.au

10 9 8 7 6 5 4

A catalogue record for this
book is available from the
National Library of Australia

ISBN: 9781922806611 (hardback)

The author acknowledges the Traditional Owners of the land on which this book was
written, the Arakwal people of Bundjalung nation, and pays her respects to Elders past,
present and emerging.

Cover and internal design by Emily Thiang
Back cover author photograph by Gabby Secomb-Flegg/Ambedo Photography
Typeset in Baskerville
Printed and bound in China by C &C Offset Printing Co., Ltd.

For my baby girl.

Growing you, while writing this,
has been the greatest blessing of my life. x

Contents

Introduction

When I was first approached to write this book, I was in the throes of morning sickness. Not the Instagrammable kind either – I'm talking a spewing-my-dry-toast-up-in-the-kitchen-sink kinda sick. Add this to my usual day, which involves taking care of my two bulldogs, Lola Lou and Archie Rose (yes, like the gin), handling the joys of pregnancy (like getting kicked from the inside at 2am), and working as a writer, speaker and model from the renovated church my high school sweetheart and I live in on the outskirts of Byron Bay (you ain't never had a friend like me!) and I'm a little short on time, to say the least. The last thing I felt like doing was sitting down and writing.

But when I thought about what I wanted to leave for my daughter, still growing inside me, I knew I had to write this book. If I could leave one life lesson as a legacy for her – and for any other woman, mother, daughter or lover, for that matter – it would be this:

Put yourself first.

I'm speaking from personal experience. As you'll see throughout this book, I have 30-plus years of pleasing others before myself, and I also have six years of mentoring hundreds of women (and some men!) on this topic from all over the world.

It's undeniable that women have been praised for our self-sacrifice, celebrated for our silence and applauded for our 'good-girl' behaviours. For far too long, we've been the peace-keepers. The martyrs. The people pleasers. For me, this way of life led to years of deep-seated resentment – towards both others and myself – as I continued to put my needs, wants and desires second to everybody else's. Because that's just what we're supposed to do, right?

So I watched on as the women in my life – mothers, grandmothers, aunties and friends – all self-sacrificed under the guise of being 'good', 'kind' and experts at avoiding conflict. Which, in turn, led to burnout, depletion and bitterness. I noticed a pattern here, and it wasn't one I particularly liked – and yet, I was also caught up in this way of living, as I wasn't taught any other way. It was all I knew.

The game completely changed for me when I started to do things differently, when my only option was to put myself – my health, wellbeing, mindset, all of it – before anything and anybody else. And while, yes, it took a lot of trial and error, and some serious metaphoric skinned knees (all of which you will learn about in this book), I am writing this from a place of true alignment. And I know it's because I figured out how to back myself, my values and my life dreams. I learned how to finally put myself first.

Because here's the thing: if you won't, who will?

So, I firstly wrote this book for my little girl and filled it with the lessons I hope to leave her with as she grows. But I also wrote it for the little girl in you – and in me. The little girl who was told she was too much, that her dreams were too big, or that she wasn't enough.

It's time for a reclamation.

It's time to put yourself first.

How to use this book

When it comes to living in alignment with your values and pursuing the life you know is destined for you, a people-pleasing way of living is one of the largest barriers to entry. Consider this book your preventative measure. I have sectioned it into a step-by-step guide to work through at your own pace. Scattered among the words are activities and exercises for you to complete in your own time. Each section invites you to 'master' the practices before you move on to the next one. Take your time with it. This isn't an ordinary book!

It's one thing to read positive words on a page, have an inspiring experience, and then stick the book on your shelf to collect dust for years to come. It's another thing entirely to implement the workings of the book, so that you walk away with not just an inspiring tale of someone else's journey but also the beginnings of your own story to tell.

Please note that the stories, examples and personal experiences in this book are from the perspective of my journey as a privileged, middle-class white female living in Australia. I recognise and respect that not every person has been afforded the opportunities and life experiences I have had, and I hope that this book offers a semblance of guidance for you, no matter your upbringing or personal life journey. These teachings have resonated with many people from many different backgrounds – from places of privilege, to joining my program homeless from a car, to not being able to leave the house due to chronic illness – and I deeply believe there is something for everyone in this book.

An introduction to people pleasing

Imagine someone you love deeply. (If you were sitting in front of me, I'd ask you to close your eyes to really feel their presence, but you need your eyes to keep reading this, so let's skip that part.) This person you're imagining is someone you would drop everything for if they ever needed you. A 2am phone call in need of help? You're on it! They're doubting their capabilities or worth? Pep talk coming right up! You sing their praises, shower them with gifts and maybe carve out all of your free time to spend with them. Who comes to mind?

Now, it would be very common for you to say your best friend, partner or a family member. Maybe even your dog (I've been known to). While this is very beautiful, loving and noble, did the thought ever cross your mind to maybe … just maybe … say yourself?

If the answer is yes, then congratulations. You either:

a) Genuinely prioritise yourself, your own self-care and have likely done a fair bit of work in the personal-development arena. Standing ovation for you!

OR

b) You put two and two together that this book is about putting yourself first, so you hacked the system. Clever cookie. You also get a standing ovation.

But now, let's take our seats.

The reality is, the majority of people reading this would have had themselves *far* down their list of priorities. Putting yourself before your loved ones? Impossible! In fact, I have delivered this exercise countless times in live workshops over the years – sitting opposite hundreds of people from all walks of life – and guess how many people have actually put themselves first? Three. And each of those three had heavily invested in the work of putting themselves first.

The thing is, this way of being isn't likely innate. Or it is, until it isn't anymore. This is where we can draw inspo from babies. Yep, babies. Think about it …

Their innate need is that of survival. Hungry = cry. Tired = cry. Feeling the feels = cry, and laugh, and make those weird gurgling sounds that are only cute when coming from babies.

Now, I'm not here encouraging you to cry every time you feel hungry (although, have you met me?). And I'm absolutely not recommending a strong gurgle sesh when you want to capture an audience. But what I am encouraging you to start to think about is *why*? Why are babies so good at putting their needs first? Shouldn't wisdom teach us that, with age, we know how to do this too? Even better than when we first started out? What happens instead is a weird reverse 'Benjamin Button effect', where we start to forget our innately human needs the older we get.

There are a few obvious pieces to remember here:
- Babies can't talk. They can't express their needs through spoken word, so feeling an emotion is a sure-fire way to do it.
- Limiting beliefs don't exist yet. I can almost guarantee you a baby isn't thinking, 'Oh gosh, what will everyone think if I burst into tears right now? I don't want to wake anyone up. I'll just stay put.'
- In my opinion, the biggest piece is that babies are pure love. They are made of love. They embody love. They don't know any other way to be yet.

In time, sure, this embodiment of love will change. They will start to mirror the behaviours they see around them. Those of their parents, their guardians and their loved ones. Those of mainstream media, television and music. Those of their teachers and peers. And before long, the baby will be developing into 'inner child' territory.

But this is also when fear arises, which can manifest as feelings of self-doubt, stress and overwhelm. All which speak far louder, and in more demanding tones, than the voice of love. The key piece to remember is this: the love hasn't gone anywhere. It's still here *taps chest*. Always. We've just forgotten how to listen to it.

This is where the game changes. I'm about to hand you a (metaphoric) stethoscope. That heart of yours is going to start speaking louder and louder. And when you listen to her? Well … you're coming back home. You're finally putting *you* first.

Know Thyself

Meet the Selfs
(Doubt, Worth and Belief)

I first face-planted into rock bottom about six years ago, although at the time I didn't realise that's what had happened. On the outside, to most people, I looked like I was thriving.

I had a well-paid corporate job and spent almost five years working my way up the business ladder. I was managing publicly listed client accounts, I shopped at high-end fashion retailers and worked in a small office in Sydney's CBD. You know those corporate-zombie stares on your morning commute? Yeah, I had mine down pat. Each morning, I rolled out of bed, already in my activewear from the night before (the Kardashians taught me that one), and would go to the gym before the sun rose with my corporate gear packed in my gym bag. I took my lunch breaks at the Westfield food court in Pitt Street Mall (if you haven't ever been, think fancy-AF food court for high rollers) and, after a full day of work (strategising, creating and mainly appeasing unhappy clients – my forte), I took the hour-long bus trip back to the beautiful Northern Beaches rental I shared with my then boyfriend (now husband) Trent. Maybe stopping back at the gym on my way home.

Social time was kept for the weekends. Which was also family time. And more time to exercise. Speaking of time, I had none of it. I was the embodiment of 'busy' and I wore it like my favourite corporate dress. I was important. I was needed. I was only 25 and already wondering if this was it. Was this all life had in store for me?

When that first little niggle of doubt crept in, I was very good at ignoring it. Or, more so, pushing it down. I'd tell myself stories, such as: 'Hollie, nobody really likes what they do for work – what makes you any different?' 'You like the people you work with, and you get paid well, so just be grateful for what you have.' And, my personal favourite: 'I don't even know what it is I want from life, so of course I'll just keep going this way until an answer becomes clear.'

I liked playing it safe. Safe felt good, even though … really … it felt awful. Your typical type-A high achiever, I'd been playing it safe my entire life. My way of feeling worthy, deserving and appreciated was through achievement. (I know this now after years of unpacking it, but at the time, I was none the wiser.)

I studied hard at school because when I topped a subject, I felt worthy. I went to university because that's just what you did after school. In my mind, there was no other option. I settled into a corporate job – even though nowhere in my life previously was I interested in business, strategy or marketing – because I needed to prove (to myself, mostly) that I was an adult and I could work hard and make money. Because that's what you did, right?

It's important to recognise here that I was also grappling with generalised anxiety disorder. This is something I had experienced since I was a five-year-old girl, panicking about what would happen if I couldn't fall asleep each night. At rock bottom, generalised anxiety had morphed its way into panic disorder. I was a statistic – the one in seven women moving through life with an anxiety-related condition.[1] At the time, I was also seeing my therapist. This was something I had done consistently from my early teens, sitting with the school counsellor (remember those rake and sandpit Zen games they had on their desk? Such a vibe). But still, I felt empty, without purpose, lost.

1 https://www.beyondblue.org.au/media/statistics

Living out of alignment

I wonder if you can relate to this sense of disconnection. Maybe for you it isn't about work at all – but something, somewhere in your life, feels disjointed. Like you *know* deep down there is so much more for you – more love, more adventure, more joy. But it's not enough to have that knowing if you don't know what to do with it, right? That's what I thought, too. So it got worse *before* it got better.

I started to suffer Sunday-itis. No, not Monday-itis. I was scared of Sundays. Because Sunday felt like so much pressure. I resented Mondays with such force that even the day before became filled with dread. I knew what Sunday night meant – another emotional breakdown, confessing to Trent 'I hate my job' like I was the worst (and only) human in the world to ever utter those words aloud.

Then, I'd throw myself straight back into it. Panic attacks became a daily occurrence. I've lost count of how many times in the office I'd have to remove myself to have a breakdown. I became very good at using my time on public transport to cry (big glasses are a must) and pulling it together, for the most part, between those partitioned walls.

I'd always been good at putting on the happy face. (I think I owe that partially to my excellent tooth-to-mouth ratio equating to a larger-than-life smile.) Happy-face-Hollie is my go-to when coping with distress. Trouble at home? Smile through school. Soul slowly dying because I'd forgotten what it meant to actually live in alignment? Laugh it off and grin through it. In fact, there are likely past clients or team members reading this who had no idea how bad it was. I became very good at pretending. I didn't know any other way. Universe forbid I actually admitted I was unhappy. Why? Because that meant I would likely hurt people.

In my mind, I was trapped. I couldn't leave my job because the team 'needed' me, my clients 'needed' me and I 'needed' to make money to support my life with Trent. If I really, truly left and put my happiness and wellbeing first? Well, then, obviously I would let everyone down, I'd be the most hated gal in Sydney's CBD and all of my family and friends would see me for what I was – a fraud, who was nothing without her achievements.

Letting go of martyrdom

I see these concerns time and time again – especially with women. There's this weird martyrdom thing we do – often unconsciously – and somewhere along the way (likely mirroring behaviours from our parents), we start to self-sacrifice in the name of being a 'good' person. Mamas are excellent at doing this. Putting themselves at the bottom of the priority list because that's just what you do, right? But *why*? Just because something has always been done a certain way, it doesn't mean it's the 'right' way for you. It's taken me five years of deep personal work to figure this out.

And, as I write this, with a baby growing in my belly and a fire in my heart (also, baby is a fire sign, so I've got some extra flames at play here), I want to challenge the norm of societal standards. No longer will I martyr myself to a job, a friendship or a societal ideal. No longer will I glorify self-sacrifice in the name of being the 'good' girl. The good mum, the good friend, the good wife, the good *insert your identity label here*.

You know what actually feels really good? Living in alignment with your values, your truth and what lights you up. That shit doesn't just feel good … it feels expansive. Inspiring. Exciting!

'But *how*, Hollie?!' I hear you cry. 'Tell me your secrets!' You're in the right place, reader. Even if you're reading this with your giant sunnies set in place on your long-ass commute to your soul-destroying job, I see you. I've been you. And I'm here to teach you that there is another way.

Exploring your limiting beliefs

To kick things off, let's get to know *you* more. What makes you tick, what makes you cringe and, most importantly, the stories you are telling yourself that are becoming your reality. For example, in my life so far, it's very clear that there were a few key 'stories' at play, holding me back from making any real changes in my life. You might like to call these your *limiting beliefs* – the stories placing limitations on what it is you believe to be true about you and your current version of reality.

These limiting beliefs are always fuelled by one of the following 'selfs':
- Self-doubt: 'I'm not good enough,' 'I can't do x, y, z,' or, like my earlier example, 'I don't know what I want from life, so I'll just stay put.' Self-doubt is debilitating. It's the voice in your head telling you all of the reasons under the sun why life isn't safe and why you're not capable. If self-doubt were a friend, they'd be draining AF.
- Self-worth: This sneaky-little 'self' is obsessed with validation, attention and feeling deserving. When we are fuelled with self-worth, we are more inclined to act on inspiration without question. When our self-worth tank is running on empty, we're more inclined to say things such as, 'Yeah, that's all well and good for you, Hollie, but good things don't happen to me like they do to other people.' Sounds like someone needs a little pep talk! Self-worth is a literal birthright – something we are all entitled to. Yet, under the guise of perhaps humility, but more likely deeply rooted guilt or shame (we'll get to that in Chapter 3), our self-worth stories are like a traffic controller holding a very large, very red STOP sign, right on the edges of our current reality and what our dream life could be.
- Self-belief: The antidote to self-doubt and self-worth. We like her – she can stay. Self-belief is the voice in your head (perhaps she sounds like Oprah, or is that just me?) telling you that you are deserving, capable, smart and enough. Right now. Just as you are. Find that one hard to get your head around? Don't worry, me too. For now, just understanding these concepts is enough. We will be working with them for the next little while, so recognising when they arise is all that is necessary.

The idea here is that now you have more awareness of the voices of the 'selfs'. You may find that they are running the show. Notice the part of you that is not actually any one of these voices – you're the observer instead.

So when you hear the voice of self-doubt creeping in, saying, 'I could never run my own business,' you, as the observer, can witness this with loving compassion. Maybe you'll even say 'hi' to self-doubt. Invite her to pull up a chair. Get to know her. You might even contemplate why she is telling you this story.

Likewise, you will start to witness the moments self-belief drops in. Maybe she's throwing you a solo dance party to celebrate an epic achievement, or perhaps she's eyeing you in the mirror exclaiming, 'Girl, you look goooooood!' Again, observe her. What are her motives? How does it feel to be in her energy?

ACTIVITY: **Meet the selfs**

Become aware of your selfs and the stories they are telling you over the coming days. Observe what arises and capture everything here.

Self-doubt tells me:

Self-worth tells me:

Self-belief tells me:

Becoming aware

I first became aware of the voices in my head at peak rock bottom.
(Note: I was still in denial about said rock bottom at this point. I just
assumed everyone felt as crappy as I did every day and nothing would
ever change that.)

I was completing one of those personality tests that you're often asked
to do in 'business land' as a way to profile the type of person you are.
On starting, we were told that there were no right or wrong answers.
Of course, high-achiever me knew that was a lie to throw us off scent,
so I gave the test my all.

When the profiling company phoned us to give us our feedback, mine
went as follows: 'Hollie, you're obviously a high achiever and very good
at x, y and z ...' *So far, so good,* I thought. *Tell me something I don't know.*
'... but I am slightly concerned by how much you worry.' *Wait. What?*
'I'm sorry, I don't think I understand. You're telling me I worry a lot?'
I asked in what I can only assume now was a hyper-defensive attempt
at dismissing negative feedback. 'Look, I think it's best you speak to
a professional,' she replied gently. I agreed, all the while playing it
'totally-unphased-but-wait-a-second-I'm-very-phased'.

I took my 'unphased-but-actually-totally-phased' demeanour home
with me that evening and brought it up with Trent with a giggle. 'Can
you *believe* she said that I worry too much?' I laughed. 'I mean, yeah
I get stressed about things, but everyone does!' To which Trent replied:
'Hollie, I tell you this all the time. You worry about everything.'

Therein lies the exact moment my face made direct contact with
rock bottom.

I decided to prove everyone wrong and show that I was actually cool,
calm, collected and any other 'c' word you can think of to describe a
chill demeanour (ooh, there's one). The next day on the commute to
work, I started to write my 'worry list'. Not dissimilar to the Meet The

Selfs activity, I started documenting every worry-fuelled thought or question that crept in.

The list grew and, by lunchtime, pages of my notebook were filled with worries.

It included little things such as:
- What if that client I have to speak with today is aggressive again?
- I really want another holiday but we don't have enough savings.

And medium things such as:
- What if I'm not good at sex and Trent gets bored of me? (Genuine concern of mine at the time, people!)
- I really want to go to Sarah's birthday this weekend, but I feel so sick and run-down.

And not-so great, big things (that took up the most space) such as:
- What do I do about work? I don't like my job and I have no idea where to go from here.
- What happens if I have another panic attack on the bus?
- What if I get home from work and find our dog dead? (Literally, it was a daily concern of mine. Specifics of her death were also different each day. Remember, I was also grappling with an anxiety disorder.)

Written down on paper, staring back at me, was a laundry list of vibes I was carrying around each day. And none of them were great. No wonder I was tired, sad and stressed. So, I did what I knew I needed. I got help.

My healing journey

I upped my Mental Health Treatment Plan to receive more therapy. We spent our sessions unpicking why the people pleaser in me was putting everyone's needs before my own to the point of a complete and utter nervous breakdown. With help from my GP and naturopath, I started a health and supplement regimen to manage my stress levels, which at the time had amounted to acute adrenal fatigue. I had to stop all exercise and rest every spare moment I had, which meant actually creating spare moments to rest. I missed birthdays and celebrations, and took more sick days in five months than I had in the previous four years. I lost friends. But even more, I lost myself. For a time, my life consisted of moving from my bed to the couch (sometimes with Trent carrying me). Friends would come and binge-watch *The Hills* with me on the weekends I was lonely. I was pretending everything was 'fine', until I gave myself permission to admit it wasn't.

At this time, I started curiously observing the personal development world. I grew up with a mum who covered our fridge in affirmations and had a bookshelf filled with Louise Hay and Wayne Dyer self-help books. So, I started reading. A year or so earlier, when my dad was diagnosed with cancer, I had discovered the work of the late Jessica Ainscough – who was known as the 'Wellness Warrior' – and was rabbit-holing myself down paths that today seem like no-brainers, but six or so years ago were pretty new (or were to me, at least). I wanted my dad to get better, so I became a woman on a holistic-healing mission. We started juicing, I experimented with chia seeds and quinoa (I even started my first wellness blog – Cooking With Coconut – to capture my rogue creations) and I began meditating.

What I hadn't yet explored, however, were even simpler concepts such as affirmation work and gratitude practices. To me, they'd always seemed way too simple. And, for most of us, when something is 'too simple', we often dismiss it. It wasn't until I had no other option but to give this 'positive vibes' thing a go that everything started to drastically change.

Enter stage left, Dr Masaru Emoto. In his bestselling book, *The Hidden Messages in Water*, Dr Emoto shares his studies in water consciousness. (Bear with me, reader – this is where things get interesting.) Also known as the 'Water Experiment', Dr Emoto performed a range of experiments on water. He used positive spoken and written affirmations (things like 'I love you' and 'You are worthy'), played the water various types of music (from healing to heavy metal) and even used low-vibrational language (think 'I hate you' or really, anything spoken by self-doubt). The molecules of water that were spoken to kindly formed the most incredibly breathtaking crystals. Those that were spoken to poorly rarely formed – they were dirty and not too nice to look at. (You can see for yourself by searching 'water experiment' on YouTube.) What Dr Emoto's experiment illustrates is that words and music have a direct impact on the molecular structure of water.

But why does this matter? Why am I all of a sudden talking about water? (Other than a nice little reminder to get your daily hydration in!) Because up to 60 per cent of the human body is water. We *are* water. (Or, like that meme doing the rounds – we're cucumbers with anxiety. But I prefer the former!) The words we speak and think literally form our reality. They are what we become. Again, when I first saw this experiment, it seemed too easy. So I kept searching.

It wasn't long before my next teacher appeared – enter stage right, Louise Hay (what a line-up!). I picked up my mum's copy of her book *You Can Heal Your Life* and devoured its pages. A metaphysical teacher, Hay's work captured everything I knew to be true in my heart but hadn't yet found echoed outside: that there is a level of responsibility for most of what we call into our lives. That if we get clear on what our thought patterns are, we can rewrite them. And that when we rewrite our stories and speak to ourselves differently, our lives start to change. I still remember working through this book for the very first time, dedicating an entire journal to it and a week away at a retreat in nature. I was committed to making it work. The former me that thought talking kindly to myself was 'too simple', 'too hippie' and 'too out there' had become a gal that had literally no other option. I could stay stuck, unhappy and bruised (from the face-planting and also the ego) or I could change.

ACTIVITY: **Self-talk**

Once you have captured your 'self-stories', it's time to get clear on the language you are using towards yourself and how it makes you feel. The good and the not-so-good. Remember, this is a space for you to observe, rather than judge.

The words I speak to/about myself that feel good:

The words I speak to/about myself that don't feel good:

The power of gratitude

Once you're clear on your self-stories, it's time to rewrite the not-so-good ones. The easiest way to do this? It all begins with gratitude. Harvard Medical School released an article in 2021 claiming that in positive psychology research, gratitude is strongly associated with greater happiness.[2] In fact, research has shown that the act of feeling grateful has a number of profound effects, ranging from cultivating

2 https://www.health.harvard.edu/healthbeat/giving-thanks-can-make-you-happier

positive feels to improving health and dealing with adversity. Most high achievers with any sort of daily wellbeing practice will count gratitude as a top-tier must – from Oprah to Richard Branson to Steve Jobs and, hey, let's throw myself in there for good measure.

It's a hard job to start reflecting on what you're grateful for when you truly don't feel grateful for much, but just like practise makes strength (not perfection, because we don't strive for that anymore, do we friends?), practising gratitude consistently over time has a profound impact on your state of mind. I remember vividly the first time I started practising gratitude. I was on a crowded bus, early in the morning in bumper-to-bumper Sydney traffic, with absolutely no energy left to be standing on a bus, let alone getting through an entire work day. And yet, I whipped out my phone and wrote in my Notes three things I was grateful for that morning:

- I am grateful for my home.
- I am grateful for Trent.
- I am grateful for Lola (#crazydoglady).

Each morning, I repeated this exercise. I'd replaced my morning gym sesh with a brain-loving sesh instead. And before long, it became easier. I was able to reflect on the little things in my day I was grateful for. The beauty of the sunrise at the bus stop before work. A laughing fit with colleagues that made my cheeks hurt. A cuddle on the lounge after a big work day. So while externally life hadn't drastically changed yet, I started to create a reframe. I was seeing the good again.

I started that practice six years ago, and it is one I continue to use to this day. I *swear* by it and its simplicity. Often, when it comes to working on ourselves, we are met with one of two main excuses: 'I can't afford it' and 'I don't have time'. The beauty of a daily gratitude practice is that these excuses don't exist. Today, my gratitude practice is a daily voice note to my bestie. We share our gratitudes, experience joy together and it holds us each to account in the practice. While right now, you may not see how being grateful is one of your ultimate tools to finally putting *you* first, all I ask is that you have trust in the practice.

ACTIVITY: **Daily gratitudes**

Start a daily gratitude practice by acknowledging three things
you are grateful for each day. Share your gratitudes with someone
(your children, your lover, a bestie) for extra accountability.

Some tips:

- Try to mix up the gratitudes each day. Thankful for a friend today? Think of someone else tomorrow.

- Play with the ways you express gratitude – try your journal, a voice note or the Notes in your phone. Bonus points when the gratitude practice is spoken aloud.

- Start to take note of the instances each day that spark a grateful feeling inside of you – when are you feeling most grateful?

Stick to at least three, but you can't OD!
The more, the better!

CHAPTER 1 **SUMMARY**

Your takeaways:

- Become aware of your 'selfs' and the way they speak to you.
- Capture the words that feel good, and not-so-good.
- Start your gratitude practice.

Stretch targets:

- Watch 'Water Experiment' by Dr Emoto on YouTube.
- Read *You Can Heal Your Life* by Louise Hay.

Next, we're diving into all things 'the reframe'. That is, once you're clear on your limiting beliefs and stories, how can you rewrite them and, more importantly, create change that has staying power?

CHAPTER 2

The Reframe

When it comes to resistance in putting ourselves first, a major belief I see – in myself and others – is that surely this makes us a selfish person. How can we possibly prioritise our own happiness and livelihood while remaining humble, loving and kind? Isn't self-sacrifice a far more noble conquest?

Let's take a look at Merriam-Webster's dictionary definition of 'selfish'.

Definition of selfish (adjective)

1. Concerned excessively or exclusively with oneself: seeking or concentrating on one's own advantage, pleasure or wellbeing without regard for others.
2. Arising from concern with one's own welfare or advantage in disregard of others.
3. Being an actively replicating repetitive sequence of nucleic acid that serves no known function.

Definition three aside (don't say I've never taught you anything!), I think it's important to highlight the energetic undercurrent of what it actually means to be selfish. While, yes, there is a component of 'selfishness' seeped in putting you first, above all, it's clear that selfishness is defined when it comes to the intent of the act in question. Specifically, these pieces:

- Without regard for others
- In disregard of others

Now, reader, I can almost guarantee that if you are reading this book right now, you're not a selfish person. People pleasers are innately driven by a deep regard for others. It's why we please in the first place, right? We want people to feel comfortable, to get along, to keep the peace – even when it's to our own detriment. This is why we choose to stay in the job we've long outgrown or spend time with the draining friend rather than taking much-needed rest. We feel uncomfortable in prioritising our own needs. We'd do anything to avoid being seen as someone with disregard for others.

Ironically, there are many conversations in personal development circles that suggest people pleasing itself is actually the ultimate selfish act (nope, not a typo), because it can be seen as a form of manipulating others to accept you or a version of you that actually isn't authentic. Woah. Mic drop. Anyone else's mind blown at that one? So, if you're concerned at appearing selfish in finally starting to prioritise you, I ask you to come back to your intent. Are you choosing to put yourself first – and doing it at all costs – even when it may intentionally hurt or cause harm to a person? Or, are you choosing to put yourself first because you know in doing so, your energy will thrive and you will have far more to give to yourself and others?

Often, our experience of what it means to be 'selfish' is dictated by the stories others share with us throughout life. There have been countless times loved ones have called me selfish for even the most minor of things, from saying no to an outing I genuinely didn't want to go to because I wasn't feeling well to screening a phone call and waiting for when I actually felt present to give that person my energy. 'Selfish' gets slapped on as a label to almost guilt someone into prioritising others over themselves. And when we do that, we are telling ourselves that that person is far more worthy of our own energy, time and love than we are.

When you're constantly labelled as selfish for acts that are actually an assertion of boundaries (this is a good thing! More on that to come), the lines get blurry. And if you're anything like me, you do whatever you can to avoid that label. You stay in the soul-destroying job or relationship. You put up with poor behaviour to avoid rocking the boat. You do whatever it takes to duck and weave the criticism that comes when putting yourself first – because when a loved one labels you as selfish, it can feel like a direct attack on your worth, value and, I'd even go so far to say, how loveable you are (especially when this messaging comes from a parent).

ACTIVITY: **My selfish story**

Take a moment now to capture your own definition of what it means to be 'selfish'. When you have this written down, recognise whether this is a story that is serving you and your life or hindering you.

Is this my true belief or something that I am mirroring from others?

Unpacking your selfish story

These stories we have formulated, which are so deeply intertwined in our self-worth, lend themselves to massive resistance – should we ever *consider* putting ourselves before others, a visceral response can happen in the body. Our palms get sweaty. Our knees get weak. Maybe our arms even get heavy. Physiologically, our bodies engage in a fear response and we'd much rather continue doing things the way they've always been done (I repeat: insanity) than risk the discomfort of trying something new (where the growth happens – on the edge of our comfort zone) or, even worse, being outcast by our loved ones for living differently. We are wired for connection, so when that connection feels jeopardised, it also feels unsafe to do things differently. The risk – although on paper may not read as extreme – creates resistance in the body.

When we engage in something for the first time, neurologically this can signal to our brains that we aren't safe and are at risk of 'loss'. An article by Scott Mautz titled 'Science Says This Is Why You Fear Change (and What to Do About It)'[3] highlights that when we feel uncertain, the brain can register it as an 'error'. To feel comfortable again, our impulse is to re-establish equilibrium by correcting that error.

So, when it comes to actually putting ourselves first and practising a new way of living, these warning signs will be fired off – creating deep resistance and all sorts of stories running wild, trying to keep us safe.

We know now that our stories become our reality. We are our stories – literally each day we choose to narrate each 'scene' of our lives, and then wonder why things aren't playing out the way our hearts desire … when the answer is really simple. We need to write a new script! Which is all well and good if you genuinely know which way you'd like your story to go.

If you're anything like I was, it's more likely you have very little clarity on exactly how you want things to look – and far more clarity on how you don't want them to look. I knew I was unhappy in my job. Heck,

3 Scott Mautz, 'Science Says This Is Why You Fear Change (and What to Do About It)', Inc.com, https://www.inc.com/scott-mautz/science-says-this-is-why-you-fear-change-and-what-to-do-about-it.html

all of the warning signs were there loud and clear. My body was unwell and drained. My mental health was suffering. I was going through the motions of my life, without any clear direction as to what was coming. Even my family and friends were telling me to leave my job. If I was into 'signs' back then, as I am now, I was getting every single one in the book. Honestly, my guardian angels at the time would have been flabbergasted. They really had their work cut out for them! And yet, the story running on loop at this time (there were many, but this one was narrated exceptionally loudly) was: 'Well, I don't know what it is I want from my life, so I will stay put (read: stuck) until I "figure it out".' Let's have a look at what was really fuelling that story …

The Five Whys technique

Enter centre stage, Sakichi Toyoda – Japanese inventor and founder of Toyota Industries Corporation (shout out to my first-ever car, the Toyota Echo – can recommend). Toyoda created a technique we use in 'root cause analysis' – that is, identifying the root belief, or cause, behind an issue – known as the Five Whys technique. It has been such a profound tool in my own unravelling that I reference it any time I come up against my own limiting stories.

When working with the Five Whys technique, it's easy to overcomplicate things. Especially my high achievers. We want to get the answer 'right'. I feel you. I see you. I am you. But I ask that, in this exercise, you remove as much judgement towards your answers as possible and allow your heart to offer up what it feels with each prompt. The process is quite simple and self-explanatory – we're going to ask 'why?' five times consecutively around a particular limiting belief or story in order to identify the real root cause of that story. Because when we start pulling at the roots, the clean slate we are desiring becomes far more accessible and beautiful new stories have the space to bloom. So, let's take the Five Whys technique for a spin with one of my own examples.

My limiting belief: 'Well, I don't know what it is I want from my life, so I will stay put (read: stuck) until I "figure it out".'

- *Why?* Because it's too difficult to make any changes when I don't know where I'm going to go next.
- *Why?* Because if I leave before I know, then I probably won't find a job or I'll end up without money or stability, which scares me.
- *Why?* Because I'm worried I'll make the 'wrong' decision and regret leaving to find something new.
- *Why?* Because I've put so much time and effort into studying hard, going to uni and spending years in this job – it will feel like it's all gone to waste.
- *Why?* Because I'm afraid of failure, and getting this 'wrong' will mean I've failed.

Boom. Fifth 'why', and we've got the juice. I wasn't staying put because I didn't know what was next. I was staying put because I was so afraid of failure, and getting the next piece 'wrong', that I'd rather sit in feelings of anxiety, depression, physical pain and energy zaps. Because failure meant I wasn't achieving. And achievement was how I felt worthy. Do you see how each story we are telling ourselves is steeped in a deeper cause? A belief, fear or 'shame' story that is dictating our every move?

Research by Dr Fred Luskin[4] of Stanford University recognised that, on average, we have around 60,000 thoughts a day – with 90 per cent of those repetitive. It's even been found that of these repeated thoughts, 80 per cent[5] are negative. Think about that for a moment, knowing that our thoughts, and words, become our reality. If most of our thoughts are going on a loop – without any conscious effort to recreate, reprogram and repattern – is it any wonder they feel like deep truths?

We'd like to think we're the narrators of our own life stories, however, more often than not, sneaky subconscious beliefs are running the show. They're great at shape-shifting and convincing our conscious mind that these stories are facts. Spoiler alert: they're not. And the most exciting part? We can rewrite them.

[4] https://www.forbes.com/sites/christinecomaford/2012/04/04/got-inner-peace-5-ways-to-get-it-now/?sh=5aed24d06672
[5] https://tlexinstitute.com/how-to-effortlessly-have-more-positive-thoughts/

ACTIVITY: **Your Five Whys template**

It's your turn to put the Five Whys into practice, using the template below as a reference to come back to. For now, let's focus on the limiting beliefs that are holding you back most when it comes to putting yourself first.

They might be something along the lines of:

- I people please because I prefer to avoid conflict.
- I don't put myself first because it feels selfish and I'd rather prioritise others.
- I feel uncomfortable when putting myself first.

Once you are clear on one or two of your limiting thoughts, let's have a go at 'Five Whys-ing' it (a newly coined term I'm sure Toyoda would absolutely support).

My limiting belief or story is:

- Why?

- Why?

- Why?

- Why?

- Why?

Herein lies the juice. Keep this handy, as we will be working with these root causes in a moment.

Five Whys technique FAQs

Q: I'm stuck at the third or fourth why and can't get to the fifth – am I doing it wrong?

A: Not at all. If you feel the answer you've landed on is your 'root', then great! You'll know it's a root cause if reversing the root is the solution to your limiting belief. (So, in my case, reversing my root fear of failure would be: 'I'm not afraid of failure', which is the perfect solution to the limiting belief I started out with!)

Q: I've gone past five whys and I could just keep going – is that okay?

A: Try to be as succinct as you can in your why responses. However, if your answers aren't igniting a feeling of emotion, or recognition, then continue until you have the root. You can also do more than one Five Whys exercise for the same limiting belief. There could be multiple roots at play here!

Q: I'm finding it really difficult to get started. Am I doing it wrong?

A: Not at all. Perhaps this is a better exercise to talk out aloud with someone you trust – a friend, family member or therapist. Remember, the aim here is to unlock those subconscious programs running the show – identifying them *is* hard. Go gently.

Creating the reframe

You know what's great about this part right now? You cannot un-know what you know. And knowledge is power. So now, my friend, you are officially seated in the power seat of your life. Although it might not feel like that just yet. Heck, we've just identified all of the shitty ways we talk about ourselves, to ourselves, on the reg. If we were our own bestie, we'd be having a seriously tough conversation right now (more on that to come!).

But this *is* exciting, as it means you have done the hardest part – the heavy mental lifting. You've become *aware*. Aware of your mindset and how it's running the show. Aware of some sneaky roots that perhaps got a little too tangled for your liking. Aware that these programs you've been running can be changed. Welcome to conscious and empowered change, reader. You're back in the driver's seat (Toyota Echo, or not!). So, now that we have this laundry list of our own limitations, what do we do with them? Is awareness enough? If only. While awareness is key, yes, unless we do something *different*, we are just going about the same old motions expecting things to change. And we know how that ends, don't we?

Now that we've sourced these little roots, we need to weed them out. Just like your garden bed or veggie patch, new seedlings need to be planted, watered, fertilised and nourished with sunlight, shade and maybe some music or a nice talking to (I'm surely not the only one talking to my plants here?). This is where we create the reframe. Consider the reframe the exact opposite belief of the root cause you've just identified. We want this reframe to be so drastically different to that nasty root that, before long, we start to embody and believe it more than the sneaky shape-shifting subconscious mind. We are literally rewriting our stories. We're flipping the script so the story goes far more like we envisioned.

Now, at first, reframing is going to feel super far-fetched. You're likely not going to believe the new statements you come up with, but that's the point. We are actively rewiring that subconscious mind and directing it to new thought patterns, which then impact our behaviours, feelings and emotions. And this is where the real game changes – this impacts your entire life (no biggie!).

The power of positive affirmation

When I first stumbled across affirmation work, I doubted it could do anything for me. How could something as simple as a positive sentence or two completely change the way I was feeling about my life? It all sounded well and good, but I had some serious physical, mental and emotional challenges at play here – a few positive sentences surely weren't going to do the job. I couldn't have been more wrong.

Enter, Claude Steele – a social psychologist who founded the self-affirmation theory, a key psychological theory behind the impact and effectiveness of positive affirmations.[6] This theory confirms that yes – at a psychological and even neurological level – affirmations are effective. There are even studies that have traced the receptivity of certain neural pathways when people practise affirmation work.[7] So, why do we resist the simple things that work?

For me, I like to overcomplicate things. Put it down to the high achiever in me that likes to work really hard to achieve results (so satisfying!). I carry a deep-seated root with me that anything worth having won't come easy (be right back, gotta Five Whys that one!). When I hear how practices such as gratitude or daily affirmations can have such a profound effect on my wellbeing, on all levels, I get suss. Even cynical. I highly doubt that it will work for *me*.

Maybe you can relate to this? I see this with the women I work closely with too. As I said earlier, our greatest barriers to entry when it comes to working on ourselves are often one or two of the following excuses:
- I can't afford it.
- I don't have the time.

6 https://positivepsychology.com/daily-affirmations/
7 https://positivepsychology.com/daily-affirmations/

The thing about positive affirmation work is that these two excuses don't exist. Repeating a positive sentence or two costs nothing and takes very minimal time and energy – much like our gratitude practice from earlier in the book. (You're still going with that one, right?) And yet, we can still resist it. Which means what we're likely resisting, instead, is change – which is the antidote to everything we are experiencing. We *want* things to change, right? It's why you're reading this book! So why are we so afraid of it?

This is likely the time for you to take a little Five Whys breather and uncover your own personal resistance to change. There are a multitude of reasons why we resist what we know we are actually desiring. Here are some of them:

- I'm afraid that if things change, I'll lose stability.
- If I become a new version of myself, my friends or family won't love me anymore.
- What will people think of me?
- I don't feel strong enough to handle any big changes right now.

Deep down, change often activates the fight-or-flight response in our bodies, regardless of whether that change is positive or negative. Often, our bodies can't tell the difference. Physiologically, we're firing off all sorts of uncomfortable signals – our breathing shallows, our stomach drops and we start to mirror feelings of stress or anxiety. Now's a great time to remind you that the sensation of excitement in the body mirrors the sensation of anxiety – they feel the same – and those feelings aren't necessarily the most comfortable for us.

In short, change can feel dangerous – even the most subtle of changes. It's a primal instinct. And the antidote here is to remind ourselves we are safe.

ACTIVITY: **Your safety zone**

When do you feel the safest? Perhaps it's spending time with a loved one – your partner or a certain friend or family member you can really open your heart with. Maybe you feel safest when expressing yourself creatively, or having a warm tea in a cosy corner at home (I'll take peppermint, please!). Often, we are so strung-out in the fight-or-flight response that the simple act of pursuing feelings of safety can be enough to shift gears. We're no longer forcing our way uphill in first gear – we're cruising along a coastal scenic drive in auto.

Start to carve out daily space in your safety zone of choice.
From these feelings of safety, we will do the work of reframing.

ACTIVITY: **The reframe**

Let's start by taking a few deep breaths together. Breathe in through your nose, and let go through the exhale. Allow your shoulders to drop, your jaw to unclench and, hey, even take your bra off and let things settle (if that's your vibe!). By now, you should be sitting pretty in that beautiful safety zone. If not, take some time to shift those gears, deepen the breath and come back to this exercise when you feel settled.

Below, capture your roots from your Five Whys exercise earlier:

We will only work with one or two roots at a time – knowing that you can repeat this exercise as often as you like, forever! There's no rush. Life is a marathon, not a sprint (thank you for that gem, Dr Phil). We're after lasting change here, and that takes slow, steady consideration.

From your list, identify below the root causing you the most challenge:

With this root is your opportunity to plant a *new* seed. We've weeded it out – there's space for a new beautiful flourishing bloom. What seed are you choosing to plant in place of this root? What is a new positive belief or story you are ready to start embodying?

Tip: try and flip the root to its exact opposite as an easy new belief to work with.

Here are some positive affirmations for people pleasers that might give you some ideas:

- Life flows when I put myself first.
- I lovingly say no to things that do not light me up.
- I only say yes to things I truly want to do.
- I find joy and expansion when I step outside of my comfort zone.
- Change and growth excite and inspire me.
- I am capable of big, beautiful things.
- I feel energised when I rest.
- I enjoy creating space for me.
- When I create space for me, I attract new opportunities and experiences.
- I feel excited, inspired and motivated by the new.
- I am worthy of my own love, time and energy.

Now that you have your *new* story, start to reflect on how you will water, fertilise and give love to this seed so it can grow. Here are some ideas:

- Saving your new seed (affirmation) as the background of your phone or computer.
- Writing it down in your morning or evening journalling practice.
- Repeating it to yourself throughout the day any time a negative belief emerges (I like to call this the 'circuit-breaker').
- Sharing it daily with a friend – speaking it aloud to someone you trust.
- Writing it in lippy on your mirror (if you do this, please share with me!).
- Creating it into artwork, using it as a central statement for your vision board.

The most important thing here is that you stay committed to this new story. Think about how you can embody the feelings of this story more in your day-to-day life. How will your life change when you start to really believe this to be true?

Your takeaways:

- Become aware of your selfish story and how this is serving and hindering you.

- Complete your first Five Whys exercise, with a focus on the limiting beliefs holding you back from putting yourself first.

- Find your safety zone and commit daily time to drop into feelings of safety.

- Create your reframe and start to practise your new story daily.

Stretch targets:

- Continue using the Five Whys and reframe exercises throughout the duration of reading this book any time a limiting belief or self-sabotaging behaviour emerges.

- Continue weeding and replanting your mental garden as a regular habit.

Next, we're talking high vibrations, baby! Get on those flares, pop on a pair of oversized sunnies and wave your arms around like a hippie at Woodstock. Things are about to get groovy!

CHAPTER 3

High Vibrations

I've always been a glass half-full kinda gal. It's been one of my signature moves for as long as I can remember. If we were getting into a nature versus nurture debate (let's save that for another book), I'd strongly argue that this is innate.

I've never been any different. I was born this way. Thank you, chairperson and Lady Gaga. (Then I'd sit down, shuffling my palm cards furiously and nodding aggressively to my fellow debaters.)

While yes, silver-lining Hollie can see the beauty in this trait – I'm always able to find something to be grateful for, I can always see the lessons in the life challenges I've been dealt and I'm pretty good to talk to in a crisis – what I've also come to realise is that often, us glass half-fullers are also likely to give freely from said glass … until there's nothing left for us to drink, leaving us a little bitter, not to mention very thirsty.

Should versus want

While writing this book, my publisher asked me to fill out a new author's form – like a getting-to-know-you type of interview. When I got to the piece on 'hobbies and interests', I froze. What do I actually *do* for fun? It was pretty eye-opening for me, because I'd like to think I'm a fun gal. But when I sat there pondering, *does hanging out with my dogs and husband count as a hobby?*, I realised I still had work to do.

Now, I am self-aware enough to know that my resistance to cultivating hobbies stems from overdoing it in my former 'put everyone first' life. At school, I said yes to every extracurricular activity you could think of. Debating team? Sign me up. Netball and touch footy? I'm in (even though, really, the anxiety that stemmed from competitive sports left me dreading my weekends). And why not umpire netball while I'm there and coach a young beginners' team too! Heck, let's throw in choir for good measure (those 7.30am before-school starts were a goody) and how about I also put my hand up for any and every leadership activity while also excessively studying (I was known to take my study notes to the netball courts) and working in our local bakery after school and on Sundays.

I took this perky school-spirit energy into life outside of school. I spent my already-very-limited time outside of work volunteering for the Make-A-Wish Foundation, spending my weekends visiting sick children in hospital and attending fundraising events as their public speaking officer. I had time to give, and I wanted it to be in service to those who needed it. I also cultivated a wide-ranging array of physical activities – everything from aerial yoga and pole dancing to boxing.

Hobbies five years ago? I had them nailed. Today? I'm resistant. Why? Because, on reflection, many of these extracurricular undertakings were from a place of 'should' rather than 'want'. I thought I should join the debating team because I was a good public speaker and my friends were joining too. Did I *want* to be spending my Friday nights as a 16-year-old girl debating the political issues of the time at local high schools? Nope. I remember the dread of those Friday nights. The FOMO of missing parties. But I was the 'good girl' – she debated; she didn't party.

I thought I should don the caps of umpire and netball coach while also playing – I was already out at the courts for the morning, so why not give up my entire day? Did I *want* to be spending 8am–4pm every Saturday running from court to court, being verbally abused by players and parents alike? Not at all. I would have much preferred a sleep-in and maybe a bit more time to study (the nerd thing is apparent now, isn't it?). But I knew my skills were valued, and needed, so I committed.

And so it continues … I thought I should join the school choir because a few friends had, I can carry a tune and the teacher really liked having me as part of it. Did I *want* to be getting to school early and practising? No. Not even a little bit. I was even ashamed to tell people I was *in* the choir (no judgments here – remember I was a prepubescent gal trying to find her way in the world. The choir–debating thing really wasn't serving my street cred). I thought I should volunteer for the Make-A-Wish Foundation, as my boyfriend was working away from home so I had more free time on the weekends to 'give' to a cause. I thought I should, I thought I should, I thought I should …

This way of living leached itself into every other area of my life. 'I *should* catch up with Maggie, even though I feel so drained after spending time with her, because she is really struggling and needs me …' 'I *should* fit in that extra gym session this week, even though my body is screaming at me to rest and I'm coming down with a cold …' 'I *should* stay put in the job I'm working at, even though I'm having panic attacks to and from the office each day …' The 'shoulds' are the issue here. Where are you 'should-ing' all over yourself? And how is this impacting how you are showing up in your life?

Now, our shoulds are not to be confused with our responsibilities. Do I *want* to be cleaning up after my dogs? I mean, it's not that fun a time, but it's a responsibility I have. (I can almost sense baby in my belly laughing right now – 'Mum, you don't know what's coming!') Do I *want* to be spending a chunk of my time sorting through my accounts, finances and bills? I mean, I kind of enjoy it (#nerd) but I also kind of enjoy a long lunch with friends … however, this is a responsibility of running a business, so I commit. We see the difference, yes?

When I started to recognise I was living from a place of 'should' versus 'want', it changed the game for me. Where are you actually doing what it is you genuinely *want* with your life? When I say want, I mean things that excite, inspire, motivate and feel deeply fulfilling. In a journalling exercise I shared with a group of women I am mentoring at the moment, I offered them the simple journalling prompt of: 'I want …' Literally, that's it. When it came time to share, there wasn't a dry eye on the call. Because when we allow ourselves to *want*, we are connecting with something far deeper than our mind. Our mind is should-ing, while our heart is wanting, desiring, calling in. And how often do we honour our heart?

ACTIVITY: **What do you want?**

Like Ryan Gosling in *The Notebook*, it's time for us to build a house
(joking). But it is time for us to question what it is we actually want,
right now, at this point in our lives. But before we do that, let's start
to identify the 'shoulds'.

Where in your life are you showing up from a place of 'should'?
This could be hobbies, work, certain relationships, exercise ...
Capture them all below, including any 'stories' surrounding
the 'shoulds'.

Now, if you were to start acting from a place of *want*, what would look
different? Perhaps start with that very simple prompt: 'I want ...'

Now, can you identify the gaps? Where are your shoulds steamrolling
your wants? And what are some *action* steps you can take to gently
introduce more wants into your world?

It's apparent I need to do this exercise myself, too, given my hobbies right now are made up of puppy cuddles and husband time (which truly, I do want, so I'm okay with that). But also, I want:

- Creativity and more play. I want to try new things such as pottery, painting and art – just for the fun of it.
- To start singing lessons! Maybe not the liturgical hymns I sung in school choir, but I'd love to be able to nail a karaoke rendition of something that isn't Eminem's 'Lose Yourself'.
- More connection with like-minded people – social time spent with new friends, doing new things.
- My health to flourish and thrive as I grow my baby girl. I want to take in more sunsets, stretch more and really prioritise my wellbeing.

Now, I have a list of my new priorities. Nowhere on this list have I said I want to self-sacrifice for the sake of others. Nowhere on this list have I said I want to spend hours of my day mindlessly scrolling and comparing. Nowhere on this list have I said I want to spend time with people who drain me.

Our heart *always* knows. But how often are we listening to it? Why is it easier for us to live from the shoulds versus the wants? Guilt. When we're should-ing, we are guilting ourselves. 'I should, because she needs me …' 'I should, because that's what's expected of me …' 'I should, because I have the time to spare …' People pleasing is fuelled by guilt. If we didn't feel guilty for saying no or asserting boundaries, then gosh things would be easier, right?

Feelings as energy

Let's take a look at guilt as an energy. In his book *Power Vs Force: The Hidden Determinants of Human Behavior*, bestselling author Dr David Hawkins developed the Map of Consciousness, which is a map identifying the various levels of energetic frequency we can experience as humans and how certain frequencies vibrate higher or lower on the scale than others. You can read more about it in his book[8]

8 hhttps://www.amazon.com.au/Map-Consciousness-Explained-Actualize-Potential/dp/1401959644

The Map of Consciousness Explained: A Proven Energy Scale to Actualize Your Ultimate Potential.

On this scale, guilt is listed as the second-lowest energetic vibration that we can emanate, coming right after shame. So, with that in mind, it has been evidenced that the two lowest energies we can embody aren't actually fear, sadness or even grief. They are shame and guilt. How often are you choosing to please someone else from a place of one (or both) of these energies? It's not a particularly nice feeling, is it?

What we know about energy is that if like attracts like – as the law of attraction states – then living from a place of shame and guilt (hello, shoulds!) is perpetuating an endless cycle of exactly that – more shame and more guilt. It's why, even though I was doing all of these seemingly noble, wonderful things with my time – the volunteering, the extracurricular activities, the social sacrificing – I wasn't being filled up in the slightest. I was feeling more drained, bitter and disappointed in myself than ever before.

These energies are running rife, as this way of living has been normalised. Burning ourselves out to complete and utter depletion? Been there, done that and can name multiple others who have done the same (including you, am I right?). Self-sacrificing to the point of utter resentment – be it for our family, our children, our friends or the stranger in the street asking for our time when we're really in a rush but we feel guilty saying no and so we spend 20 minutes nodding politely at their spiel on why you should donate to their local charity of choice? (Or is that just me?) Common. Happens all the time. Working a job that is destroying your spirit? Heck, even the terms 'Monday-itis' and 'TGIF' point to the collective disparity with working a job you dislike (but hey, you get weekends and four weeks of leave a year, so it's worth feeling flat and resentful for the majority of your time, right?). Very normal conversation point. In fact, now that I work a job I truly love (being your own boss is a vibe I will never tire of), I've felt a serious disconnect from the masses and their relationship with work, and even my own sense of guilt for actually enjoying what I do in exchange for money. How warped is that?

The point is this – guilt is running the show right now. Collectively, it's far more socially acceptable to complain about your job, your relationship, the lack of time you have, your recent nervous breakdown, the supplements you're on to support your adrenals and the fact you have no time whatsoever for yourself than it is to claim you have a spacious, inspired and abundant life without having to self-sacrifice.

In fact, this collective belief of sacrificing yourself (for what I still don't really know) is so normalised that those going 'against' the grain are often shamed. They're the 'dreamers' with their heads in the clouds. They need a 'reality check'. They're the exception to the rule. But what if these beliefs were just more sneaky subconscious thoughts running the show? What if it was actually very doable to start living life on your own terms? Not eradicating guilt or shame entirely (we are human and are meant to feel it all), but becoming more aware of these energies and how they feed in to the choices we are making in our lives? How could we choose to live a little differently?

I'm glad you asked. The answer is simple – joy. Yes, joy. One of the highest vibrations on the scale of consciousness, under only peace and enlightenment, seeking joy as a circuit-breaker to counteract shame and guilt is one of the most consciously rebellious acts you could opt to invest your energy and time in right now.

I know what you're thinking (I'm an intuitive, remember?): 'How can I possibly experience any joy with the personal challenges I'm experiencing in my own life?'

One of my dear friends, Joyful Mentor Nicola Ayres, shared a beautiful notion with me recently: that even in times of darkness, we can lean on joy to bring us hope and faith. Even when things feel murky, heavy or challenging, we can still seek joy in the smallest of moments and ways. Consider it your antidote to shame and guilt. So, what does joy look like for you? Let's dive in …

ACTIVITY: **Joyful, joyful**

First, let's get clear on what joy *feels* like in your body.

_____

When you are in a state of joy, what are the physical and emotional responses that emerge for you? Perhaps you smile so big your cheeks hurt, or maybe you feel a sense of peace and ease. Take a moment now to jot down the feelings you associate with being in a state of joy.

Now, have a think about the people, places and activities that bring you these feelings – they leave you feeling joy. Capture them all here:

For me, I experience joy when:

- I'm listening to inspiring, uplifting music and dancing around my home.
- My husband comes home from work and we spend time connecting at the end of the day.
- I'm having a belly laugh with my good friends.
- I'm sharing delicious, good food and a cocktail (well, mocktail right now) with loved ones.
- I've taken a trip somewhere new.

Now that you have your joyful list, we're going to carve out *more* time to feel these feelings. Because when we're in joy, guilt and shame are no longer running the show. They may still rear their heads – that's okay – but now you know how to send these energies a little more love and give them a little less airtime.

Finding flow

Positive psychology – the study of living a 'good life' (sign me up!) – emphasises the importance of seeking joy in our days through flow-state activities. Mihaly Csikszentmihalyi – the positive psychologist credited with identifying flow as a necessary component of mental wellbeing[9] – recognised that when we are in a state of flow, we are fully immersed in the activity at hand, allowing our full presence and involvement in the exercise. This is where ego and fear are more likely to drop away, and we are therefore more open and receptive to positive feelings.

To be considered a flow-state activity, the following boxes must be ticked:

- Full immersion in the task at hand – that means losing yourself and feeling disconnected from time (there's no rushing, checking the clock or watching time).
- An element of challenge – this helps with task immersion, as well as occupying the mind (and perhaps distracting it from thoughts).
- Something that you enjoy and look forward to – there has to be that level of *joy*!

Yes, reader. You're hearing me correctly. Your task right now, should you choose to accept it, is to start cultivating more activities that leave you in a state of flow. (If now isn't the time to take up chess, I don't know when will be!)

ACTIVITY: **Go with the flow**

Write down all of the state-of-flow activities that come to mind, regardless of whether you have an interest in them or not. Use the dot points on the previous page to ensure they tick all the elements of being in flow (for example, while a beautiful act of self-care, a bubble bath ain't that challenging, friends!).

———————————————————————

Once you've got your list, go back and highlight the top three–five activities that get you excited. List them here:

Try not to overthink these practices. If you have limited time, how can you incorporate dance and music into your household chores? Can you switch off Netflix an hour earlier to prioritise reading before bed? Can you swap your daily social media scroll with cooking cinnamon scrolls instead?

Here are my simple daily flow-state activities:

- Pumping 'high vibe' music and dancing/singing along every chance I get – showering, washing the dishes, breaks between writing (listening to music alone isn't flow, friends – we've got to add that 'challenge' through movement or singing along!).
- Writing – and not just this book (although it's my favourite form of flow!). Journalling, writing poems in the Notes section of my phone, creating content for my business – my nerd flag waves wildly at this one!
- Meditation – while hard in the moment at times, I feel joy once I have sat in my practice. Sometimes your flow-state activities may feel like a bit of a chore (like your daily walk or jog, or maybe the preparation it takes to get creative in the kitchen), but you'll always feel much better for it afterwards.

And there you have it – your flow-state list of feel-good fun. It's time to introduce one (or more) of these activities every day. It doesn't have to feel hard. It gets to be fun! We've been taking it all way too seriously for far too long now. Let's lighten up a little, shall we?

CHAPTER 3 **SUMMARY**

Your takeaways:

- Become aware of your wants versus your shoulds – where are shoulds running the show?

- Get clear on what you want (what you really, really want!).

- Start to identify moments of joy – the feelings, activities and moments you feel most in joy.

- Create a list of flow-state activities and commit to practising one (or more for my high achievers) every day.

Stretch targets:

- Sign up to that class, course or new hobby you've been putting off from fear – the ultimate way to call in more joyful vibes.

- Seek out books and teachings by Dr David Hawkins – I highly recommend *Letting Go: The Pathway of Surrender.*

Let's take a big, deep breath in – fill your belly – and sigh on out. You're doing incredibly well so far. You have just dived in to a level of self-awareness that most people avoid at all costs. Because rather than being laced with sunshine and rainbows, this work *is* confronting. When we look at our deepest fears, the beliefs that have held us back for a long time and that pesky voice of self-doubt, it's not always a nice feeling. I want to commend you for showing up regardless. Because guess what? Even in just committing to this work, you *have* started to put yourself first! And now that your self-awareness is on tap, we can start to journey down the winding road of purpose, alignment and deeply embodied fulfilment. It's time to get to know your values.

Know Thy Values

CHAPTER 4

The Compass (Values) and Road Map (Alignment)

I was having a conversation with my husband this morning. We were talking about a friendship we had both recently noticed a shift in – a slow increase of distance and feelings of guilt around the 'should-ing' of spending time with them.

Now, the catch here is this friend hasn't done anything 'wrong'. They are a wonderful person with a pure heart and lots to offer in a friendship. So, why do we feel this disconnect? Well, our values are no longer aligned.

For any new parent-to-be, I'm certain you can relate. All of a sudden, the weekends fuelled by binge-drinking and emotional D&Ms until the wee hours of the morning are replaced with emotional D&Ms discussing the politics of a Bugaboo purchase versus a hand-me-down stroller from Cathy down the road. For single Sally (let's call her that), that conversation is boring AF. Sally can't relate. Sally probably doesn't even *want* to relate. I get it! I was Sally just a year ago. But now, it's literally all we think about.

Therein lies the change. What once used to tie our friendship together – a mutual love of margaritas, a go-go-go energy and 'hustler' mentality – has been steamrolled by our blatantly obvious and very new differences – early nights, prenatal vitamins and a very skilled ability to spew on the side of the freeway (no hangover in sight). Our values are now different to Sally's. And that isn't a bad thing. It points to changes, yes, but there is no one to blame.

Now, for you, this may not be playing out in the 'becoming a new parent' realm – although maybe you're the Sally in this dynamic, going 'Righhhhht – this is me right now. I haven't done anything wrong.' No, Sally, you haven't. In fact, you're likely staying true to your friendship values while your friends navigate the newness in theirs.

Perhaps it has nothing to do with parenting. Maybe you've started your own side hustle and your new values of freedom and entrepreneurship have you connecting on a deeper level with other self-employed trailblazers. Or maybe you've emerged from the 'spiritual closet' and are now openly owning your interests in oracle cards and numerology. Of course, connections will adjust accordingly. You're valuing spirituality in a new way – it's now a priority for you. I remember when I started stepping more into practices that were aligned with my spiritual beliefs and a friend told me, 'No offence, Hollie, but I don't believe in any of that stuff you bang on about.' Again, a rejig of values – for us both. And this one ended up becoming a deal-breaker in the friendship.

Living in alignment

Consider your values the compass, and living in alignment your road map. To follow your path – your true north – you will never be led astray when you are living in alignment with your values. It's when your values are prioritised in your relationships (friends, family, partner), career, home environment, health (mind, body and soul) and the list goes on. The trouble is, most of us are trying to navigate a road map with no directions, compass or GPS. (Remember a time before those?) Is it any wonder we don't know where we're going most of the time?

But, before we get clear on our values, what is all this 'alignment' talk about? While yes, in this metaphor, our values are represented by a compass facing true north, when I refer to alignment here, I'm talking about far more than walking in a straight line. Living in alignment – in a spiritual context – refers to living 'on purpose'. That is, you're living your life based on your purpose, vision and ideals for the life you wish to lead. Alignment runs much deeper than looking a certain way, although you can absolutely tell when someone is living in alignment. They are the person who has that 'energy' – things just happen for them and they are energised, vibrant and enjoyable to be around. When you spend time with someone in alignment, it can feel inspiring, motivating and act as a reminder of your own innate potential.

Underneath the outward appearances, however, alignment comes down to embodying a *feeling*. Or perhaps a multitude of feelings. For example, I know when I am aligned based on a few key factors:

- I feel deeply energised and inspired in my days (one of my highest values is inspiration).
- Opportunities seemingly fall in my lap out of nowhere.
- I notice serendipity in life as well as synchronicities and signs, such as feathers, ladybugs and angel numbers (hello trusty 11:11!).
- I receive beautiful positive feedback from clients, friends and strangers – affirming that the traits I admire in others are also within me.

Overall, alignment feels *good*. It feels on purpose. On path.

Understanding your purpose

Now, if you're someone who gets totally in their head about what their purpose is, welcome to the club. Pull up a seat. Get comfy. Because I'm about to make your life so much easier. Your purpose? It's to be love. Yep. That's it. Not a job title or marital status in sight.

Flashback to the baby talk at the beginning of this book. We are born from love. Energetically, as babies – before society drills into us who we 'need' to be – we are pure love at our core. *That*, my friends, is our purpose. To return to love. How do we do that? We live by our heart. Easier said than done, I know. How can one possibly listen to their heart after years and years of constructing a giant double-brick wall around the perimeter of their heart space, only lowering the drawbridge every now and then for a knight in shining armour waving a red flag? I hear you. Let's go gently, shall we?

ACTIVITY: Listen to your heart

It's time to start connecting with that beautiful space in the centre of your chest. Below, I have written a guided meditation practice. You can also download it http://insighttimer.com/hollieazzopardi to listen to in your own time.

Take a moment to get comfortable. Comfort looks different on everyone – perhaps your eyes are closed, maybe you're sitting with a candle lit or lying down with an eye pillow. Just take a moment to set up now.

Once comfortable, start to connect with your breath. Breathe in deeply through the nose, fill your belly and really let go on the exhale. Try that twice more here – breathe in deeply, and sigh out.

Now, allow your breath to settle in its own natural rhythm. There is no right or wrong way to breathe. Just allow the breath to move naturally through you. Notice how your body settles as your mind softens, and how peaceful it feels to relax into the breath.

Very gently, take your awareness to your heart space. That is, the very centre of your chest. Start to direct the breath gently here – breathe deeply into the chest, and let go on the exhale. Perhaps you feel called to imagine you are breathing in light – maybe it's a beautiful pale-pink colour, like a rose-quartz crystal, or green, which is the colour of the heart chakra. Maybe a different colour entirely. Just allow this light to expand – rippling through your heart space and opening up your energetic centre. If an emotion arises here, allow it to move through you. If you're getting caught up in your thoughts, that's also okay – just come back to the breath.

Now, placing a hand or two on your heart space, I invite you to ask it, 'What do you need from me in this moment?' Listen to and trust in whatever comes first. 'What do you need from me in this moment?'

Take a few more moments here to breathe consciously with the wisdom that has landed for you today. When you are ready, you can start to deepen the breath – in through the nose, out through the mouth. As you bring gentle movement back into your body, send deep gratitude to your heart space for this wisdom received. When you feel ready, you can open your eyes.

Now, while the wisdom of your heart is still fresh, take a moment to capture anything above. It might be a feeling that came up for you – a word or two – or maybe a whole page of wisdom. Whatever feels right for you.

The wisdom of your heart

Welcome to the wisdom that lies in your heart. Energetically speaking, the heart space is the keeper of profound wisdom. The centre of the seven chakra points (the energy centres in our bodies), the heart acts as the bridge between the human and the spirit. Our heart, while regularly referenced in rom-coms and James Bay ballads, is so much more than a space of romance and heartbreak. Alongside our gut, our heart is the home of our intuition. Our heart is the space of passion – and not just sexy passion (although, here for it!), but also passion for life. Our heart beats for us every damn day without question. It is our life-force and the keeper of love for ourselves, others and the beauty of the world around us.

The trouble in connecting regularly with our hearts lies in the societal celebration of the logical mind. To listen and live from your heart is, in this day and age, quite a rebellious act. Because no longer are you outsourcing your deeper, innate 'knowing' to a news source, politician or parent proclaiming they know what is best for you. Guess what? *You* know what is best for you. It's time to trust in that more.

Now, in lots of spiritual circles, you may come across the notion of 'silencing the mind'. I'm here to give you permission to ignore that message. In my opinion, that's *way* too much pressure and why people are so quick to turn their backs on practices such as meditation and living more in tune with your intuition. Rather than silencing your mind, can you just start to turn down the volume? Because when you do *this*, you allow the volume of the heart to increase. Our heart gently whispers to us. It doesn't demand attention. While the mind may yell, the heart steps back and says, 'I'll be here when you're ready.' It needs space to communicate with us. This is why practices such as flow-state activities, daily gratitude and affirmation work all have the power to disconnect you from the noise in your mind and drop you back into the depth of your heart.

Consider your heart the gatekeeper of the path your soul desires to walk down. No matter what obstacle, roadblock or red flag comes your way, when you listen to your heart, you will never be led astray. (And it rhymes, so you know it's true!) Honestly, Captain Planet had it sorted when he gave one of his Planeteers the power of 'heart'. It is your superpower, to bring you back into that beautiful space of alignment.

ACTIVITY: **Aligned and alive**

What does alignment feel like for you? In this activity, we are working with *feelings*. So rather than getting caught up in what your purpose, alignment or values *look* like, our focus right now is how they make us feel.

Think about a time in your life where things just flowed – life had ease and excitement. Opportunities maybe landed in your lap, relationships flourished – including your relationship with yourself – and you showed up in life as your 'best self'.

How did that time in your life *feel*? Capture all of the feelings you can come up with below:

Note: If you cannot recall a time in your life where you have felt aligned, bring to mind someone you know who you see as 'living in alignment'. What feelings do they embody?

Now, with this list of feelings, can you write down the top three–five that feel most inspiring for you right now? If you were to seek these feelings every single day, what would they be?

Fake it till you make it

Great, now it's time to do just that. This is where I encourage you to fake it. Yep, we're faking it till we make it. I'll let you in on a little secret – no one knows WTF they're doing. Truly. I'm writing my first book while growing my first child, with absolutely no idea what I'm doing on both fronts. But I'm showing up anyway and winging it. Just like I've 'winged' my successful business, solid relationship and much of the experiences I've called into my life.

I'm very good at pretending until it becomes reality. And this is what we are doing with our vibes. Yep, our energetic vibration is going to shift based on our ability to fake it. Your body cannot determine the difference between you waking up naturally vibrating at 'joy' versus you pumping *Sister Act Two*'s 'Joyful, Joyful' as a little jump-start into joy. What matters here is that we are clear on the vibes we are seeking each day and the ways we can cultivate them.

ACTIVITY: **Feel the vibrations**

Referencing your top three–five list of ideal feels from the previous page, can you start to identify certain activities you can do, people you can spend time with and ways to spend your days that will allow you to cultivate more of these feelings?

For example, one of my aligned feels is inspiration. So, for me, my regular practices that cultivate feelings of inspiration include:

- Culling my Instagram feed and only following accounts that leave me feeling inspired (also, Mute is a vibe).

- Singing and dancing along to music that evokes emotion.

- Having a beautiful office set-up that inspires me to work – with flowers, oracle cards and a natural outlook (plus a super-plush pink velvet armchair).

- Conversations with friends who inspire me, documentaries on people who inspire me (most recent fave is the Billie Eilish doco – #recco!) and interviewing people for my podcast who I find inspiring.

For you, maybe it isn't inspiration you're seeking. Maybe it's play, joy or energy. There's no right or wrong. For now, just get super clear on those key feels and how you can seek out more of them in your day.

You may find in this exercise that many of the feelings of alignment you are seeking are also embodied in your flow-state practices. Doubling up is very normal here – you're not doing it 'wrong'. What's happening is you're recognising the practices, places and people that leave you feeling in flow, in joy and in alignment. And *this* is how we start to get clear on our values.

Accepting our humanness

But before we dig deeper into values, it's important to note the very human aspect of this work. In Dr David Hawkins' Map of Consciousness, he didn't just highlight the high-vibrational emotions, dismissing anything sitting under 'neutrality' on the scale because feelings such as grief, fear or anger felt uncomfortable. In fact, you will see that the scale highlights just as many high vibrations as those feelings measured as a lower-vibrational frequency. Why? Because we are human. Yes, 'we are souls having a human experience' – or however that Instagram quote doing the rounds goes – but so often we can get caught up in the 'soul' that we become frustrated with the 'human'. But to be human is to experience the *full* spectrum of emotion. That means that in any given day – heck, any given hour if you're anything like me – we can go from joy to grief to peace to shame and back to joy again. This. Is. Normal. I repeat: This. Is. Normal. (And also a great time for you to watch *Inside Out* – because apparently Pixar movies are made for adults now?)

Please do not 'high achiever' yourself with this one. Trust me, I know all the tricks. You may look at the Map of Consciousness, reflect on all you've learned to date and your mind might get a little sneaky and start whispering, 'You should really be operating at joy or peace as often as possible, because they're two of the highest vibrations. Otherwise, you're failing.' Or is that just me? The 'failure' in this work is actually in dismissing the human that arises in experiencing a full spectrum of emotions. We *want* to feel everything – the stickier feelings like grief and guilt have just as much a place at the table as peace and love. All are welcome. Rather than running from them, how can you let them in?

Harvard neuroscientist Dr Jill Bolte Taylor claims that it takes approximately 90 seconds to identify a feeling and let it pass.[10] Let that land ... 90 seconds. So why is it that feelings can seemingly linger for days – sometimes weeks – without budging?

The first trick lies in actually *allowing* ourselves to feel what we are moving through. The challenge here is that so often we don't

10 https://www.alysonmstone.com/90-seconds-to-emotional-resilience/

because the feelings are uncomfortable. We don't want to cry or, Universe-forbid, have a nervous breakdown in the middle of a corporate meeting (although can confirm, it won't kill you. Also, can confirm there is much to be said about taking a breather in a bathroom stall at the office when said breakdown is imminent). We don't let ourselves feel things because that means discomfort and, sometimes, heavy emotional pain. This is where we don't have to go it alone. I see a multitude of emotional-support practitioners who help guide me through the 'stickier' emotions that are often connected to deeper traumas, challenges and stories that are very hard to unpick on your own. Here are some of my favourite healing modalities.

Therapy

Sitting opposite a therapist, psychologist or counsellor is a wonderful way to unpick the stories, childhood traumas and challenges you may be experiencing that are connected to emotional discomfort. The key here is to seek out a practitioner you trust deeply. For me, I also appreciate a practitioner with a holistic approach, incorporating meditation and mindfulness techniques, as well as loving compassion.

Kinesiology

Using a technique known as 'muscle testing', kinesiologists are able to access the subconscious mind, identifying programming, stories, patterns and perhaps even traumas you are unaware of. Using a combination of energy-clearing techniques, they are able to release these stories from your subconscious. Feelings *will* arise in these sessions; however, they move through you quickly as you are held by a professional.

Emotional Freedom Technique (EFT)

EFT utilises a series of 'tapping' points on various meridians (energy channels) in the body to move stagnant energy through your nervous system and physical body. I've sat in EFT sessions and cried, laughed and even burped (no kidding, it's apparently a thing!) – these are all ways your body can release stored emotion through gentle, supportive practices.

Neuro Emotional Technique (NET)

NET is another technique evidenced to help process trauma and stagnant emotions through the body. Guided by a chiropractor, this technique focuses on the physiological roots of the traumas to release emotions from the body.

Havening

If it's good enough for Justin Bieber, it's good enough for me! Another stress-relieving technique involving gentle touch on various points of the body, the Havening Technique works in calming down the amygdala and generating anti-stress responses in the body. It's a beautiful practice of self-soothing.

Reiki

Reiki originated as a holistic therapy in Japan in the late 1800s. You may know it as an energy-healing technique. Promoting deep healing states of relaxation, rest and emotional release, a reiki practitioner will work on the energy centres of your body either via distance or in person, using their hands as you lie and receive.

The most important thing to recognise here is that when feelings or emotions arise in everyday life that don't budge in a 90-second 'feel the feels' sesh, then you have options. You don't have to do this alone. Part of living in alignment is allowing yourself to seek help and guidance to activate more of the juice that comes from feeling the full spectrum of the human experience. It's known as the law of polarity – for any heaviness we feel, there is just as much light on the other side. It's so important we don't ignore the heavy because, in doing that, we are also dismissing the fullness of the light ahead.

Please note: If you are experiencing any mental illness or more serious health or wellbeing concerns, seek professional help in the form of a psychologist or counsellor. Energetic and healing modalities should always complement your mental health treatment of choice.

ACTIVITY: Feel the feels

Here's a technique you can use any time a sticky emotion arises that feels a little uncomfortable. We are going to be actively feeling the feelings by working with the understanding that once we identify and allow ourselves to fully connect with the feeling we are experiencing, it is more likely to move through us. Before we start, make sure you are comfortable and in a setting that feels safe, and have your journal handy to capture what arises for you.

If you would prefer to listen to this guided practice, check it out here: http://insighttimer.com/hollieazzopardi

Find a comfortable position – perhaps you are lying down or sitting up with your back straight and your neck free to move. Whatever feels best for you. When you feel ready, close your eyes.

Take a few deep belly breaths here – breathe in deeply through the nose, and allow the breath to be released as a sigh on the exhale. Do this twice more, imagining that you are releasing any stress, tension or overwhelm as you exhale.

Now, allow your breathing to settle – dropping into its natural rhythm, however it wishes to move. Very slowly, take your awareness to your mind. Can you be the observer of your mind? Notice the part of you that is not your thoughts – the part that is witnessing them. Can you witness these thoughts as they move through you with loving compassion? Can you be gentle with yourself as you observe these thoughts and their movement?

Now, imagine you have a little dial on the edge of your mind – this is the volume dial. Can you start to very gently turn down the noise of the mind? Perhaps it doesn't disappear completely – but can you just allow the noise to soften slightly?

When you feel ready, start to use the breath to seek out any points of tension, resistance, frustration or pain in the physical body. Where are you drawn to? Simply be the observer here once more. Can you use the breath to send energy into these points of tension?

When discomfort arises, your most natural response would be to move away from it. Here, know it is safe for you to breathe deeply into the discomfort. Do not run from it. Breathe in deeply, and allow the breath to gently shift any of this heaviness or stagnant energy.

Continuing to focus on the breath and allowing it to release any tension, start to observe any feelings that are arising for you. Can you name any feelings or emotions? Again, without judgement, simply observe these as you breathe.

If you notice yourself running off with a story as to 'why' you're feeling what you're feeling, gently bring yourself back to using the breath as a release. There is no need to run off with any stories right now. Just breathe deeply.

Continue to breathe deeply until you feel a shift in your body – perhaps a shift in emotion, feelings or tension. There is no need to rush. Just breathe.

Start to deepen the breath now. If you moved through anything particularly sticky, perhaps shake out your hands or arms and move your head and neck slowly from side to side – just honouring whatever your body needs to do to shift this energy out of your system.

When you feel ready, very slowly come back to the space.

Now is the perfect opportunity to write in your journal anything that may have arisen for you – to potentially explore with your emotional practitioner of choice or perhaps capture for your own self-awareness.

CHAPTER 4 **SUMMARY**

Your takeaways:

- Practise the 'Listen to your heart' meditation daily
  – at least for this week, if not as an ongoing practice.

- Reflect on what living in alignment feels like for you,
  and identify the top three–five feelings you are seeking.

- Highlight ways you can start to actively seek out these
  feelings each day (and pursue them!).

- Use the 'Feel the feels' meditation any time a sticky feeling
  arises.

Stretch targets:

- Consider investing in additional support to help move
  more challenging emotions or energies – use the list
  provided as a starting point.

- Watch Pixar's *Inside Out* (no kidding!).

Living in alignment with your values is an act of identifying,
feeling and then embodying these feelings. Now that you are
clearer on the feelings you are seeking in your days and *how*
to move through your emotional states in any given moment,
it's time to get clearer on how to put the wheels in motion and
take inspired action.

CHAPTER 5

Foundational Practices for Alignment

I've never felt more aligned than I do in this moment, right now, writing these words to you. I'm living in a home that only a year ago I would have called my 'dream home' – the location, the land, the super-green outlook at every corner and obviously a kitchen big enough to bust my moves in while cooking – it ticks every box!

My relationship with my husband is thriving, we're expecting our first child (a miracle I do not take for granted) and our health, and that of our loved ones, is flourishing. Writing this book, honestly, has been my biggest career achievement to date (and you know how I love to achieve!). Writing down my words to share with you just lights me up like nothing else. I am surrounded by close friends and family, beautiful opportunities for growth, space for rest and a level of abundance I used to only dream of. Sounds pretty epic, right?

But what lies beneath this alignment? It's actually so much more than identifying my values, pursuing them and then, 'Hey presto, you're officially aligned!' In fact, to be honest with you, the act of living in alignment for me was far less steeped in identifying, listing and classifying my values in priority order, and far more in going out and actually *living*. Trial and error. What do I like, and what don't I like? Becoming *aware*!

The journey to alignment

I know I'm aligned in my work right now because I also know what it feels like not to be. Sitting at a partition opposite a brick wall working on other people's dreams will never feel aligned for me. Do you see how alignment here is a *feeling*? A *knowing*? An *embodiment*? In fact, I felt *more* aligned going 'back' into a retail job (after a university degree and five years of corporate under my belt – you can just sense the ego death, can't you?) than I did in those years prior, when I was making far more money and appearing far more 'successful'. This was because I had more time to look after my mental and physical health, I was able to study something I truly felt inspired by, *plus* #staffdiscount (obviously). (It's worthwhile noting that this kind of 'knowing' does not, in fact, live in your mind – rather, this feeling of alignment lives in your heart. Your gut. Your intuitive feels. You could say it passes the vibe-check!)

It's also important to note here that the process of living in alignment for me has taken multiple sacrifices and hard work. For example, when I left the corporate world, I still needed to make money. I juggled four jobs – retail, promotional modelling, freelance writing and starting my wellness-coaching business via cash jobs sitting on my friends' beds. Trent and I also moved in with his family to save on rent money. In fact, my very first 'office' was the front living room of his family home. Sometimes – in fact, most times – the journey to alignment is riddled with hard work. But when the destination is so expansive, it makes it all worth it!

Similarly, I *know* I'm aligned where we live; for the majority of my life, driving from home to *anywhere* in Sydney's CBD gave me immense anxiety. I even once had a panic attack in the Sydney Harbour Tunnel while driving – and I'm sure I'm not the only one. My nervous system suffered severely where I used to live. Where I live now, I rarely, if ever, see a set of traffic lights. I'm driving through winding country roads and stopping on the side of the road to watch baby lambs play with their mothers in fields of daisies (not even a metaphor, I literally did that this week). My nervous system *loves* living here. It feels good. It feels at ease. It feels safe.

Now, my values here aren't 'baby sheep perusing' or 'no traffic lights', but the *feelings* these instances give me are *valuable* to me. They offer a nod to when I feel aligned, and when I do not. The same can be said for relationships. I know when friendships or family connections feel aligned, as I am excited to spend time with the person, the exchange of energy feels mutual and I feel supported and celebrated. When these *values* of mine are not apparent, and feelings of resistance and resentment arise in the connection, I know the relationship is out of alignment. It's a feeling, not a list of tick-box words.

So while, yes, your values are the compass to your road map of alignment, remember we need more than a compass to get to where we're headed. We need our hiking boots (our foundational daily practices that ground us and offer support), our water bottle filled right up (the energetic practices we engage in to support ourselves and others) and when the path gets a little twisty, we need our people (self-explanatory – connection is everything).

Understanding your values

Let's start with our values, shall we?

If you asked me today to rattle off my top values, I wouldn't hesitate in listing them as these:
- Love
- Kindness
- Inspiration
- Freedom
- Wellbeing
- Spirituality

If you asked me again next week, they would likely be the same. (Maybe I'd swap 'wellbeing' for 'health' or 'spirituality' for 'soul', but the sentiment would remain the same.) But like the chicken-or-the-egg scenario (I vote chicken), what comes first? Do your values dictate your ability to live in alignment or do your *feelings of alignment* determine your values? It's hard to say, although I'm sure most personal-development mentors have an opinion on the topic! To be honest, I've lost count of how many times I've sat opposite a coach or mentor with a list of 100 'value keywords', being guided to narrow the list down. ('First, highlight any that jump out at you. Then, continue to cull until you're left with five. Boom – your top values!' Can you tell even I have run this exercise before?)

While I can appreciate the directness of this exercise, it has more often than not left me feeling more flustered than inspired. For starters, don't make me choose between kindness and compassion when they feel separate to me and, also, if I want to pick seven, let me pick seven rather than five. Also, the pressure to 'narrow it down' can feel rushed, not to mention working off a predetermined list isn't really allowing for intuitive knowing or feeling to be the guide (instead, the list acts as the guide).

Actually, that's the biggest piece of resistance for me with this exercise. It's encouraging a logical-minded thought process in deciding your values, rather than the intuitive-guided embodied reflection of your values. It's a subtle difference, and maybe not an important one for you. (In which case, go for it – I've included an example of a 'values list' on the next spread to use as a guide to narrowing yours down, if need be.) However, keep in mind that we have been working deeply with unravelling the mind. We're not 'should-ing' as much. Instead, we're being led by our hearts. And remember, the heart whispers. She deeply knows. She *feels*. She doesn't need a list.

Reflecting on the time you've spent diving deep into the feelings you are cultivating each day, the activities that leave you feeling more 'you' and the moments in your life you feel most aligned, can you start to recognise a theme in the values playing out in your life? Maybe you've noticed a pattern when it comes to physical movement – a desire for more exercise, deriving pure joy from your regular Pilates class and feeling the most 'you' when you're connecting with others at the gym or through a team sport. It would be safe to assume here that one of your values is 'health' (or 'exercise' – there are no rules here!). Or perhaps you've noticed a real desire to slow things down – to create space in your weeks to honour alone time, start a meditation practice and take more time for introspection. Perhaps a value here is 'spaciousness' or 'solitude'. It's time to reverse-engineer our values based on our relationship with alignment.

ACTIVITY: **My values**

As we dive deep into identifying our key values, I want to remind you of a few things.

Your values can change. You are an ever-growing, changing person with evolving needs. These are never set in stone and you can revisit and change them at *any* time.

They can be a feeling (such as 'joy'), an action (such as 'play') or a broader concept (such as 'Mother Nature').

These are *your* values, and you can have as many as you like. If you find you have three really solid ones, amazing! If you prefer eight because it's your lucky number (me too!), then go for it!

The main piece to remember here is that your values act as your compass to living in alignment. They are the words that guide you into the feelings of alignment you identified earlier. With that in mind, what are yours? Here is a list of core values to use as a starting point.[11] Remember to use this list as a guide, rather than anything deeply prescriptive. If a value of yours isn't on the list, that's okay!

- Abundance
- Adventurous
- Approachable
- Authenticity
- Belonging
- Charity

- Commitment
- Compassion
- Consistency
- Courage
- Creativity
- Dependability

11 https://examples.yourdictionary.com/examples-of-core-values.html

- Diversity
- Education
- Empowering
- Enthusiasm
- Entrepreneurial
- Environmentalism
- Equality
- Family oriented
- Fearlessness
- Fitness
- Freedom
- Friendliness
- Fun
- Giving back
- Good humour
- Hard work
- Health and wellbeing
- Honesty
- Honour

- Inclusion
- Independence
- Individualistic
- Integrity
- Kindness
- Learning
- Loyalty
- Open-mindedness
- Optimism
- Passion
- Perseverance
- Pragmatism
- Positivity
- Reliability
- Respect
- Social responsibility
- Spirituality
- Sustainability
- Tolerance
- Work-life balance

My key values are:

If you're struggling to identify any values at all, perhaps you'd like to start with reflecting on a few in each area of your life. For example:

My values in career are:
- Feeling inspired, motivated and abundantly rewarded.

My values in health are:
- Feeling energised, motivated and strong.

My values in connection are:
- Feeling inspired, loved and supported.

From here, you can start to narrow them down. I can already see a pattern playing out in the examples above – recurring themes of 'inspiration', 'motivation' and perhaps 'abundance' and 'love'.

Embodying your values

So, now that you have your trusty little values list, what's next? Well, these values are for you to keep close to your heart. Your values will determine when you are living for *you*, and when you are living for others.

Your values – when you're living with them at the forefront of your days – will encourage you to choose *you* in each moment. They are your secret weapon to living an aligned life – choosing *you* first.

For example, when I recognised how important inspiration was to me – being one of my top values – I started making very different choices in my life:

- I only accept work that feels exciting and inspiring to me – that means the team, project, brand and topic must ignite a feeling of #inspo. If they don't, I'm not doing it (no 'should-ing' here!).
- I prioritise spending time with friends and loved ones who leave me feeling inspired. No longer do I feel obliged to entertain gossip and judgement-fuelled conversations because that leaves me feeling the opposite of inspired and totally out of alignment.
- I invest in art for my home that inspires my creativity, I always have fresh flowers in the house (it inspires beauty for me) and I love watching TV shows like *MasterChef* and *The Voice* because I am inspired by witnessing others in their zone of genius.

Similarly, I can tell when I am *out* of alignment when I haven't felt inspired in a while. When I feel flat and uninspired, I can quickly circuit-break the blockage with an inspiring activity such as watching a sunset in nature or listening to my favourite music.

Another common value – and one I continually need to work on – is 'wellbeing'. Without my health, I'm unable to do all of the other wonderful things in my life that leave me with the aligned feelings I'm seeking. You can't feel too inspired, motivated or creative sleeping off fatigue (or the whole first trimester of pregnancy, am I right?).

But while it's a very important value of mine, is it one I actually prioritise in my days? No. In fact, my daily wellbeing practices such as meditation, movement and nourishing eating are often the very first to go when I'm feeling flat, lethargic and out of alignment. And rather than pulling myself back into the rhythm of these practices – knowing that they leave me feeling *good* – I avoid them at all costs.

This is where self-sabotage comes into play. Self-sabotage has one objective, and one only: to steer you right away from your true north. Self-sabotage wants to get you off path. Like Swiper in *Dora the Explorer*, self-sabotage *will* stomp on your hiking boots, tip out the water in your bottle and have you believe that the path you're headed down is impossible to navigate. The key here lies in knowing that self-sabotage will emerge on this path you're walking. The more aligned the path, the louder self-sab (let's give her a nickname shall we?) will speak. This is where we pull out the big guns. It's time to get out those circuit-breakers.

ACTIVITY: **Your circuit-breakers**

Reviewing your values list, have a look if any (or maybe all) of your values have some very obvious self-sab behaviours attached to them.

_____

For instance, while a value of mine is wellbeing, I know self-sab comes out to play regularly in the below instances:

- Not getting in my ideal two meditations a day – the excuse of not having time or being busy.

- Not moving my body every day – see excuses above, and repeat here for emphasis.

- Ignoring the need to meal prep and then resorting to last-minute food options that don't feel nourishing to me.

- Spending more time scrolling and binge-watching Netflix than reading a fiction book or spending screen-free time with loved ones.

Now, it's your turn.

My value:

My self-sabotaging behaviours steering me away from this value:

Some confronting truths here, right? The thing about self-sab is that we *know* the behaviours that are likely to emerge – and while awareness is the first step, yes, it's often not enough. So, referencing your behaviours above, how will you circuit-break them so that you are able to pursue your aligned path?

I'll go first. Here are my self-sab circuit-breakers:

- Setting an alarm on my phone each day to remind me of my meditation practice and actually carving out the time in my calendar to do it.
- Planning my week of movement in advance. Holding myself to account with Pilates classes with friends and, if all else fails, cutting laps around our property (read – taking a gentle waddle).
- Organising a weekly meal-delivery service so I don't have the excuse of 'forgetting' to shop or prepare meals for the week ahead.
- Using my book gift card to purchase some exciting new fiction books, and reading them in the bath before bed.

Notice that my circuit-breakers all involve taking *action*. Honestly, the thought of scheduling in my meditations each day feels annoying, but in these moments we come back to the reason *why* we are doing this. And it's to create a *new* path. To keep walking that true north path. Remember, nothing changes if nothing changes. We sometimes just need to get out of our own way.

Now it's your turn.

My self-sab circuit-breakers are:

Hint:

The Five Whys activity is an effective circuit-breaker for any self-sabotaging beliefs or behaviours. Once you have your root, pull that baby out! Spend time unpicking it with a professional, plant a new seed (belief) and watch your path start to bloom with beautiful blooms rather than wild weeds.

Same goes for your high-vibe actions – these are your aligned-feels activities, your state-of-flow moments and the people and places that ignite joy. Self-sab hates joy, flow and alignment. It can't survive in these spaces, which is just what we're looking for!

So, now that your compass is facing true north, let's double check those hiking boots of yours are in working order. Because one thing is for sure – this (life) path of ours will sometimes get a little jagged. What seems like a straight line may verge into unknown territory – maybe some inclines, steep descents and perhaps even a tumble or two. We need to make sure we're fully supported – that our foundations are unshakable, even to the very twisty turns. This is where our daily practices – the routines and rituals we cultivate each day to bring us into feelings of alignment – become non-negotiable.

Alignment in practice

I remember clearly when I first set out to live a more aligned life. I was watching a YouTube clip of a woman I admired who was claiming that if you didn't have a meditation practice, you weren't taking your creativity seriously. At the time of watching this, I also remember how much that statement triggered me and I'm pretty sure I slammed the laptop shut and didn't finish watching. At that time in my life, my habits and routines were based around getting through the day without an autoimmune flare-up, as I was still recovering from adrenal fatigue. The idea of having a regular practice of *anything* was enough to send me into a spiral of perfectionistic exhaustion. Now, with hindsight on my side, I understand what she was teaching (and the point she was getting to in the part of the clip I closed my laptop on). Our daily practices become who we are. The routines and rituals we commit to each day are what become our energetic vibration.

For example, if we are committed to a life of ease, introspection and rest, of course, it would make sense to have a regular meditation practice. Otherwise, we're not *really* taking those intentions seriously, are we? Maybe for you, you've realised that alignment feels like play and laughter – so a regular practice bringing those emotions to the forefront would be your priority. This could be something like hula-hooping to end your day or maybe seeing live comedy once a week.

Morning and evening routines are all the rage right now. We can probably recite the day-to-day practices of those we admire – they likely display them with pride in their Insta-stories (also, this is a brilliant way to maintain self-accountability #justsaying). But do they *really* need to be practices we commit to every single day? Well, it depends how much you want it. Triggering statement, right? Truly, when you're choosing *not* to do something (your daily medi, regular exercise, *insert your state-of-flow activity here*), what you're saying, underneath all of the noise and excuses, is that it isn't a priority for you. But this is where I remind you that if your own happiness, alignment and values aren't of the utmost priority to you … then what is? Are you not your biggest priority?

ACTIVITY: **Priority check**

Let's take a look at the daily practices you *already* have in place and how they highlight where your current priorities lie. Try not to overthink it, just cast a curious eye over your day-to-day or weekly habits to identify your current priorities.

I'll go first.

My regular daily habits:

- Sleep-in
- Scroll mindlessly on my phone
- Spend morning writing, emailing and working
- Check in with a friend or two over the phone
- More mindless scrolling
- Run a call or coaching session
- More mindless scrolling while watching TV
- Bed

Can we already see that my daily priorities – aka my biggest priorities right now – are rest, work, social media (*cringe*) and more work, with a side of friends for good measure?

My regular weekly habits:

- A big walk at least three times a week
- Meditation at least four times a week
- Journalling at least three times a week
- Reading a fiction book
- In-person catch-up with a friend
- A nightly bath ritual with candles, music and oils

Here, we can see that my values of wellbeing and spirituality are being slightly weaved into my week, but they're not a priority right now if we were only looking at my regular routines or habits.

Now it's your turn!

My regular daily habits:

My regular weekly habits:

My current priorities:

ACTIVITY: Cultivating new routines and rituals

Now is the chance to create *new* routines and rituals for alignment that are based on what you value and truly desire to prioritise. These could be practices you commit to daily – or perhaps weekly is enough for you right now. Again, try not to overthink it. What would feel *good* for you? When do your days/evenings/weeks feel most aligned?

Here's my ideal day in alignment with my values:

- Sleeping-in (your gal loves rest!).
- Not switching on my phone until I have completed my morning routine: meditation, journalling (perhaps with an oracle card pull) and morning stretching/Pilates/movement.
- Nourishing breakfast with beautiful music, taking my time.
- Work time – writing and creativity – until early afternoon.
- Breaking for lunch, rest or a stroll with a friend or solo (depending how I feel).
- Inspo time – reading, watching something inspiring, calling someone who inspires me, creating a vision board, taking a pottery class – the list is endless!
- Ending my day with a bath and nourishing dinner with my husband.

Do you see how the adjustments in my day, while super minor (like not switching my phone on until my routine is complete or setting aside regular time to feel inspired), make a significant change in my daily approach to feeling more 'me'? Herein lies the key to putting yourself first – you actually have to *choose you*. Every damn day. Because, I hate to be the one breaking it to you, no one else is going to.

I've especially seen this with mothers of children who have grown up and started families of their own. Enter the mid-life crisis. When you place your *entire* existence on the lives of people outside of you – even the ones you love more than anything in the world – you are forgetting that, at the end of this wild thing called life, you are truly only ever guaranteed yourself. Now, that may be terrifying for you. Especially if you prioritise everyone before yourself. If this is you, then this exercise is of the utmost importance. It's time to start becoming your very first priority. How can you choose *you*, even in the smallest of moments, each and every day?

Ideal day in alignment with my values:

Commit to yourself

Now, if you're anything like me, you'll look at your list and think the following (perhaps all at once):
- I'm so excited to have a new routine to adhere to!
- How can I possibly stick to this every single day? Doesn't Hollie know I have young children/a demanding job/a university degree? (Seriously, I ask myself a variant of this question too – who do you think you are, Hollie?)
- I'll probably stick to this for a bit and then fall off the wagon, so what's the point in even starting?

Feeeeeeels! Truly. I wrote the above list with ease because I literally *just* did this exercise myself. And while I'm excited by the potential of living my life more in alignment, I'm doubtful of my capacity to actually commit to each habit. I'm scared to 'fail' in committing, so why would I even start? I'm right there with you. Hiking alongside you. These boots may have been made for walking, but my gosh they need some breaking in, don't they?

So, that's what we're going to do. We're going to wear in these foundational routines slowly so that, over time, they become more comfortable to trek in. Because when the road gets twisty, *these* habits will bring us back to our heart – to our centre, to our truth. And *that's* why we're feeling the resistance, right? Remember, when our body senses change – no matter how positive – it screams danger. Drop back into your heart, my love, and recognise that there is nothing safer for you to do right now, in this moment, than make a commitment to yourself each day. No matter how small.

Now, it's important to recognise here that – especially as women – we are cyclic beings. Like the seasons and the moon, we move through phases – literal phases with our menstrual cycle and energetic phases whether we bleed or not. There are days and weeks when we will feel energised and willing to go for that run, take that extra class or cram in all of the social catch-ups we can muster. And, just as often, there will be days and weeks when we will feel depleted at the thought of getting up for our morning routine, let alone getting through an entire yoga class. It is so important you honour the rhythmic nature of your energetic cycles. And only *you* will know what that looks like.

A simple practice that may help you connect with your energy each day is to place your hand on your heart as soon as you wake up in the morning. Perhaps your eyes aren't even open yet. In this subtle space between sleep and wake, ask yourself: 'How am I feeling today? What do I need?' Therein lies your answer.

Recognise when your routines have become rigid and obligatory versus enjoyable and uplifting. Remember, you can change it up at any time! What matters most is that each day you find a way to choose *you* – your values, your alignment, your heart. This is the key to putting *you* first.

Your takeaways:

- Identify your key values.
- Get clear on your self-sabotaging behaviours and your circuit-breakers to counteract these.
- Reflect on your regular habits, and what these are telling you about your current priorities.
- Determine your new routines and rituals for living in alignment.

Stretch target:

- Try starting your day by placing your hand on your heart before you even get out of bed. Ask it what it needs from you. Then go and do that!

By now, you will have a super-clear idea on the feelings, practices and actions you can start taking (heck, maybe you've started already!) to cultivate more feelings of alignment. And we know now that when we *feel* aligned, we are far more inclined to choose ourselves in each moment. But what happens when we get a little 'heady' about these practices? When we find ourselves disconnecting from our heart or over-analysing our values? How do we stay committed to the path of alignment, even when our energy feels a little shaky? I'm glad you asked, because now it's time to get to know our energy.

Know Thy Energy

CHAPTER 6

Energetic Hygiene

How would you feel if I told you that everything – and I mean everything – is made up of energy? Your dog. This book. That crystal your bestie got you for your birthday last year (rose quartz?). They are all matters of mass vibrating at an energetic frequency, emitting energetic truths and responding to environmental stimuli. We are energy in constant motion.

Now's where the game really changes. How can we use this in our favour? And how is this hindering our experience of what it truly means to live in alignment?

Energetic sensitivity

I've always been a particularly sensitive person. I've cried more times in *MasterChef* this year than I'd like to admit. Growing up, my sensitivity wasn't particularly welcomed (cue: 'Oh, it must be "that time of the month"' from loved ones *cringe*). But I've also always known that, deep down, being sensitive isn't something to be ashamed of.

I'm not someone who hides my emotions – mainly because even if I tried, I wouldn't be able to. My face is super expressive. When I feel something, I let it engulf me – like a tidal wave of feeling. If I want to cry, I'll do it – on public transport en route to the soul-destroying job, in the office cubicle, at the movies. You name it, I've likely cried there. The last time I cried was during the *MasterChef* grand final last night.

My heightened sensitivity is not just reserved for opening the floodgates. I am easily excitable. I remind myself often of that Alec Baldwin character in *Friends* ('Our first fight?! This is amazing!'). I feel rage, frustration, joy, grief – sometimes all within the same hour (hormones, am I right?). Which is all well and good when the feelings you are experiencing are yours to experience.

What I realised a little while ago was that the heightened emotions I was moving through every day weren't always my own. Yep, I was picking up on the vibes (vibrations) of other people – colleagues, clients, my partner, friends, strangers sharing their unsolicited traumas with me in my DMs (it happens!). I could wake up on top of the world and then spend some time with a loved one going through a really challenging time or just open my phone and suddenly be wearing someone else's challenge alongside them like a badge of honour – all before breakfast.

For a long time, I was proud of my hyper-sensitive trait. I was an 'empath' – a highly sensitive person (HSP) – and that made me superior to others. (It didn't really, but this is truly what I felt for a long time.) I couldn't help feeling all the feels, because 'I'm an empath'. I couldn't help feeling super drained after running a workshop or attending an event, because 'I'm an HSP' (are you even a highly sensitive person if you don't abbreviate it?). It was my ego-fuelled excuse of why people drained me and I genuinely believed it made me unique, even special. To take on other people's energy as my own was the most noble of acts. It was a gift. But, it wasn't really.

This 'gift' left me avoiding social outings through fear of what I may 'pick up on' (and actually still does some of the time). This 'skill' left me resenting components of work that used to bring me joy because my energy 'couldn't hold the intensity'. And, above all else, this 'talent' was fuelling my desire to put every person before myself. Heck, I was opting to carry other people's *energy* for them. And energy – while we can't see it – is a very heavy load to bear when it isn't your own.

Perhaps you can relate to this? Maybe you even felt a big sigh of relief when you learned what an empath or HSP was? Finally, you could explain why you've been feeling drained all the time! In fact, in a workshop I ran this weekend, I asked for a show of hands for who on the call referred to themselves as an empath. No surprises that every single person put their hand up.

Here's the thing: while yes, we can be aware of this label, and proudly wear it through our days, this actually becomes an enabler to our people-pleasing behaviour. You *can* change this identifier – being the empath or the HSP. But often, we choose not to because these labels become an intrinsic part of our identity. We *like* to wear our energetically sensitive badge of honour. We feel special, unique. Which, let me tell you, you absolutely are. But, I invite you now to question if your stories around your energetic sensitivity are really serving you. Do you really, truly *enjoy* carrying the load of other people's energy for them?

Being an empath versus being empathetic

The game changed for me when I started to question the differences between being an empath and having empathy. There is a very notable difference. I would go so far as to say that the definition of 'empathy' has been totally diluted with the concept of being an 'empath'. Let's look at the difference, shall we?

empathy[12]
The ability to understand and share the feelings of another.

empath[13]
(Chiefly in science fiction) A person with the paranormal ability to perceive the mental or emotional state of another individual.

Do we see the very real differences? The ability to understand and share feelings (a level of energetic separateness) versus the ability to

12 https://www.lexico.com/definition/empathy
13 https://www.lexico.com/definition/empath

SECTION 3: Know Thy Energy

perceive mental and emotional states (deeply intrinsic). Also, we can giggle at the science-fiction reference, but how damn special do you feel when you identify as something seemingly other-worldly? If you're anything like me, we like to be labelled as the empath because it points to our intrinsic magical qualities in a very clear, concise way.

Therein lies the mass confusion – because you can be beautifully empathetic without having the energy or essence of the person you're empathising with lingering wherever you go. You can be empathetic without taking on the energetic toll of being the 'empath'. They are not a two-for-one deal. There is no hidden bargain here. The aim of this game is to unravel your identity from the empath matrix just enough to preserve your own energetic wellbeing and keep the empathetic part of you intact. It's no longer good enough to wear the weight of your loved ones' world on your shoulders under the guise of being an empath. What are you doing to shift this?

ACTIVITY: **The empath versus the empathetic**

It's time to get clear on the identifying labels we are deriving a level of self-worth from. Perhaps you have never labelled yourself as an empath or a highly sensitive person – that is okay. We are going to explore both being an *empath* and being *empathetic*. I can guarantee you've experienced at least one of these.

Let's start with the empaths. For example, when I was closely identifying as an empath, I would:

- Avoid social situations or even hosting my own large events because my energy would be left drained afterwards.

- Cry alongside loved ones going through a hard time, and really feel their stress and overwhelm to the point of debilitating worry and sleepless nights.

- Not leave the house sometimes as the energy outside felt 'too much to bear' ('pandemic energy', am I right?).

- Use 'I'm an empath' as the reason for my intuitive wisdom, and why I gave excellent guidance to my clients and friends alike.

Below, identify the ways you allow the 'empath' version of you to move through your days:

Now, let's take a look at empathetic you. For me, I recognise I am an empathetic person when:

- I show deep compassion for those struggling and offer support when my energy allows it – through time, space-holding or a charitable donation.
- I offer a safe space for loved ones to speak honestly and openly without judgement.
- I find myself in non-judgement, even when I disagree with someone's point of view.
- I connect like-minded people in communities that feel safe and supportive.
- I offer myself loving compassion, rest and gentle kindness.

Your turn.

I am empathetic when:

Empathy versus sympathy

Ladies and gentlemen, let's welcome Dr Brené Brown to the stage (and the crowd goes wild!). Now, firstly, if you haven't watched her TED Talk 'The power of vulnerability', do yourself a favour and stop reading this *right now* to go and watch it. I'll be here when you're done. (It's going to be a stretch target anyway, so there's no avoiding this!) Okay, right. Now that you're on the Brené Brown froth train (welcome!), you'll understand why anything and everything she shares is of value.

In the context of empathy, Brown notably highlights how there is a very real difference between offering someone empathy versus sympathy. She says, 'Empathy fuels connection. Sympathy drives disconnection.'[14] Why is this important? Think about it … when we offer someone sympathy, we are *feeling* their feelings alongside them. We are literally in the energetic trenches shovelling through their shit, getting our hands dirty and probably not asking for a drink of water because that would be 'rude' (just me?). To the empaths or HSPs reading this, this is likely how you're living with the people in your life that you're putting before yourself. You're in those trenches with them, disconnecting further from yourself and, quite ironically, disconnecting further from said loved ones, too.

The difference is that offering *empathy* allows you to support, hold space and listen with love without being in that trench. You're clean, energised and likely well-hydrated, which means you have *more* to give. You can reach down into that trench and pull your loved one out, without breaking a sweat. Do you see the difference?

14 https://twentyonetoys.com/blogs/teaching-empathy/brene-brown-empathy-vs-sympathy

Energetic hygiene

Our energetic hygiene is so critical when it comes to putting ourselves first and no longer allowing ourselves to be steamrolled by the needs and desires (and dare I say energetic 'loudness') of others. When not contained, our label as an empath or HSP is an enabler to people-pleasing tendencies. It's an excuse for poor energetic hygiene.

When I first started practising as an intuitive reader, I was so incredibly excited that I booked out my days with one-on-one sessions. It was very normal for me to sit opposite at least ten to 12 clients a week, mostly in the comfort of my own home (well, at this time it was the home of my in-laws – thanks for letting me hijack the living room, Russ and Wen!). It didn't take long for me to burn myself out. Again. Which, at the time, left me deeply confused, as I assumed for the longest time that burnout was only reserved for people working in corporate jobs they disliked.

This time in my life forced me to recognise that energetic exhaustion and burnout can *also* come from doing what you really, really enjoy. When you have no energetic boundaries in place, it doesn't matter *what* you're doing with yourself. You could be spending time with your favourite people or making all of your financial or career dreams come true, but without energetic hygiene or any sort of energy-preservation practices in place, you *will* inevitably reach a point of burnout or depletion.

So, what did I do to manage this period? I still *wanted* to hold my one-on-one sessions. I *loved* them, my clients and the work I was doing. But I didn't love the bed-ridden, no-exercise, vitamin B12 injection-fuelled days. I had to make some changes. This is where energetic hygiene is a matter of trial and error. What *my* energy can hold is unique to me. Similarly, your energy may be able to hold far more than mine and not feel any depletion. The first step here is to identify what energetic exhaustion or depletion *feels* like to you. From there, you can use that as a turning point for real change.

For me, energetic exhaustion feels like:

- Being super drained and fatigued after spending time on a certain task or with a certain person. You know that feeling of complete and utter brain fog and needing to lie down for the rest of the day doing absolutely nothing? Yeah, that.
- Heaviness in my limbs. My arms and legs will feel like I've run a marathon and, secret's out, your gal is not a runner. Heaviness in my limbs is a sure-fire sign for me that my energy is screaming for some rest.
- Adrenaline rushing through my body. My energy can feel erratic, stressed and overwhelmed when I haven't practised any sort of energetic maintenance. It's like a buzzing of my cells or an inability to switch off, especially when winding down before bed.
- Mood changes. I think we've all established I can feel all the feels and then some like a trooper, however I know my energy is not aligned when I am feeling emotions that are not 'mine' – they feel unfamiliar, misplaced and disjointed.
- Not being called to the practices that make me feel good. Alignment is so far from my train of thought that my values are all over the place.

Now, it's your turn.

ACTIVITY: **Energetic depletion**

Our energy communicates to us through bodily cues, symptoms and feelings that are entirely unique to us. Start to become aware of the ways your body is pointing to something being 'off', energetically speaking.

How do you feel after spending time with someone you just don't vibe with?

How do you feel after conflict with a loved one?

How do you feel about saying yes to something you wish you had just said no to?

Start tuning in to these feelings and jot them down as they arise. Before long, you will have a very clear list of the feelings and signs your body is sending you when your energy is not aligned and therefore depleted.

Tuning in

Our intuition communicates to us through bodily signs and feelings, which is why getting clear on what an energetic 'no' feels like for us is the first step to getting clear on what a 'yes' feels like. This is where the game well and truly changes. While your intuition lives in and communicates to you (for the most part) through bodily responses, signs and cues located from the throat down, your logical thought process lives in your mind. Start to get clear on the ways your body communicates a yes or a no to you. Once we have these 'messengers' clearly identified, we can start to make life choices from a place of intuitive 'knowing' versus 'should-ing' (your intuition will *never* 'should' on you, ever!).

This is where the gift of being an empath or HSP comes in handy. For you, knowing when your intuition is saying yes and when it's saying no is an easier-to-access ability. But empath, HSP or even 'psychic reader' aside, guess what? We are *all* innately intuitive by nature. Every single one of us. Yes, you reading this right now. You are an intuitive person with a brilliant inner compass designed to just 'know' things. We've just been trained to block out that little skill, mostly because in today's culture, we unfortunately still bow down to the overtly-masculine-energy way of life that is fuelled by hustle culture and a worshipping of the pragmatic and logical.

Now, that's not to say there isn't a place for logic or pragmatism. The challenge here is that this mass-collective focus on fact, science and evidence leaves us with little room or even desire to tune in to what is happening outside the noise our mind makes (or the minds of others). Because, believe it or not, you are *so much more* than your thoughts. There's a part of you – a beautiful, love-fuelled wise-beyond-your-years part – that can witness and observe your thoughts without *becoming* them.

The feeling brain

While French philosopher René Descartes famously stated, 'I think, therefore I am', Benedict de Spinoza challenged this, arguing in his work *Ethics* (1677) that the mind is not the sole function of being human, but a supporting mechanism to ensure the body's survival. Neuroscientists have since dived deep into the 'feeling brain', recognising that there is in fact validity to the claim of 'I *feel*, therefore I am'.[15]

However, because our intuition communicates softly, and historically it has not been celebrated so much in public mainstream arenas, this voice of *knowing* is often neglected. Heck, I still feel uncomfortable when I share with people that part of my work is as an intuitive reader. Even with my booked-out calendar, hundreds of beautifully positive

15 https://www.nytimes.com/2003/04/19/books/i-feel-therefore-i-am.html

testimonials and a waitlist longer than my arm to book in with me, I feel a sense of shame – because for the most part, people just don't 'get it'.

If I said I was a doctor or a scientist, especially in today's climate, I would be celebrated. When I say I'm an intuitive reader, yes, some people are intrigued (lots, in fact). However, I've also been shamed, even from loved ones who vocally doubt that what I do for work is in fact 'legitimate'. I've been in this arena long enough now to not take these words or judgements to heart. I understand that people are quick to judge and label from a place of misunderstanding or perhaps even confusion. What saddens me is that every one of us – those inside the 'spiritual closet', those waving their wands wildly and those with absolutely no interest in it whatsoever – has access to such deep wisdom. And many of us are missing out on beautiful life potential because of our resistance to dropping deeper than our minds.

Understanding your intuition

So, what *is* your intuition? Where does it live? How does it speak to you? How can you use it more? I like to think of our intuition as our voice of reason. Most choices or decisions in my life today are made from intuition. I'm talking all of them – from what I eat in a day to what I wear, the movement I do (or do not) and the words you're reading right now. My intuition guides every decision I make and I *know* that when I live from that place – of deep trust in my inner wisdom and guidance – that I will never, ever be led astray. In fact, it's no coincidence that in one of the most collectively intense periods most of us will live to experience (I'm writing this book in 2021 with most of my loved ones experiencing some form of a lockdown due to COVID restrictions), I have not felt more aligned. I almost feel guilty in saying that. While collective energy is heavy, fear-fuelled and charged by misdirected (and also somewhat justified) anger, I am sitting in my beautiful rural home, writing my first book and growing my first child with the love of my life. Truly, life has never felt better or simpler. And intuition is what led me here, with a side of energetic maintenance.

So, how do I do it? How do I remain energetically intact when there is so much 'head noise' around, telling me it's in my best interests to be fearful? I'm glad you asked. Here are my non-negotiable energetic-maintenance practices. Because when my energy is taken care of, it filters into all areas of my life – I feel grounded, I *respond* versus *react* and, above all else, I trust deeply that everything is unfolding for me as it should be.

My energetic-maintenance practices

- I prioritise rest. Now, I know what the mamas reading this might be thinking: 'Good luck when that baby comes!' And yes, I know that things will absolutely change and take some massive adjusting. But for now, rest is a priority. And rest needn't look like a nap (although, I'm here for it!). Rest can be as simple as putting the phone away (boundary) and gazing up at the sky, letting your mind settle. I would say that rest is *not* watching trashy TV or catching up with a friend. I'm talking doing as minimal as possible – focusing on simply *being*. If you are more inclined to need to 'do' something, yin yoga is a brilliant active restful practice.
- I get enough sleep. I love sleep – everyone knows it. And I feel that while we've come a little way in recognising how important sleep is for our physical and mental wellbeing, perhaps we haven't realised yet that it is also *paramount* for our energetic wellbeing. I'm the gal who currently gets between eight–nine hours of sleep a night (plus, I am growing a human so it's easier for me right now). Now, I know this isn't doable for everyone. But for those of us staying up late scrolling, watching *Love Island* (guilty!) and pottering, I say get to bed! Here are some of my favourite sleep facts (I told you, I'm a sleep nerd!):
  - The hours of sleep you get before midnight are worth far more than those afterwards.
  - The sleep hormone melatonin cannot function properly with artificial lighting, which is why at least an hour

before bed it's ideal to switch off your backlit devices, pop on a candle or salt lamp and wind down (imagine that in caveman times, our melatonin rose when the sun was setting. We want to mirror those vibes!).

- Your bed should be reserved for sleep and sex. No TV. No working from bed. Have your bedroom set up as a sanctuary – something that reminds and encourages you to unwind.

- I create space and slowness in my days and weeks. Take it from the gal who used to think a free space in my calendar meant I was available! (Note to self: it doesn't.) I now schedule space into my weeks knowing that I can only commit to *one* – yes, *one* – social outing, work event or other 'doing' activity per day. Less on Sundays – I keep them entirely spacious. Space is *key* for energetic hygiene, and it also gives you the opportunity to 'tune in' in the moment and ask what you really *feel* like doing with that time versus what you think you 'should' be doing.

- I keep to strict work hours. Working for myself, this used to be difficult, but after burnout #2 I realised I could no longer see clients on the weekend and I scaled my sessions right back from 12 a week to two. Yes, these days I only see two clients a week. I write from morning to lunchtime, and then I stop – even when I think I 'should' just write a bit more or my client waitlist is bulging at the seams and I have the space. I know what my energy can hold from a work perspective, and I don't ever overcommit.

- I limit social outings. Now this is something I've not had to really forcibly practise because I'm naturally a bit of a hermit. I love staying at home. However, moving to a new town has forced me to seek new connections (more about that in Chapter 8!), so my way of managing that right now is averaging two catch-ups a week. I make sure the catch-ups are aligned – not just in terms of who I choose to spend my time with, but also what we are doing. This means lots of beach walks, and acai bowls and chais at my favourite cafes.

- I use movement to shift energy that feels 'too much'. Especially as collective energy can be contagious. (Literally, emotional contagion is a thing. Research has documented that we *can* catch other people's emotional states[16] – you're not crazy!) When I feel stuck, sticky energy that maybe isn't mine, I get moving! Usually by popping on a playlist (I have one for every mood!) and shaking it off à la T-Swift. The moves aren't necessarily graceful – I just let my body do what it needs to do. This is also the perfect time to take a boxing class, go for a run or simply shake your body until you feel the heaviness of the energy lift.

- I include my voice in the mix too. Vocal toning is a brilliant practice of using your throat and voice to make sounds – any sounds – that release tension, frustration or 'stickiness' in your throat (where lots of stagnant energy can lie, especially for the people pleasers who feel their voice is not heard!). Pillow screaming is another sure-fire way to shift stagnant energy. While yep, you'll feel a bit crazy when you start, the release that comes from opening your voice box and letting the energy move *through*, rather than swallowing it whole, is a feeling of liberation like no other. And it also beats yelling at a loved one! Alternatively, you can just sing really, really loudly in the car – I once had a friend tell me they spotted me driving 'while yelling at someone on the phone'. Nope. I was just mid-performance. Try it (and thank me later).

- I create boundaries around my social media usage. One way to totally derail your energy? Take on the noise, opinion and emotional contagion of every single person you follow on social media. No wonder we're carrying around such erratic energies! While I dance between firm boundaries on scrolling (the ideal case for me would be not checking my phone as soon as I wake up or at least an hour before I go to bed), the regular practices I swear by are:

  - The Mute button – I go through phases of literally muting every person I follow, minus a few close friends and family.

16   https://www.psychologytoday.com/au/blog/the-empaths-survival-guide/201807/emotional-contagion-work

- The Unfollow button – something the people pleaser in me is still getting the hang of, to be honest. To make it clear, just because I Unfollow you, it doesn't mean I don't like you. Instead, it means I'm curating a feed that feels *aligned* and energetically supportive for me. There, I said it!
- The Delete button. I delete the app from my phone on the reg. It's become normal for me to take breathers for a day, a week and even months at a time (without having to announce it to the world). I feel into what my energy does when I am on the platform and, when it feels 'too much' for me, I say goodbye. Yep, even with an online business to run. I've even gone so far as to tell previous management not to position me as an 'influencer', as I never want to be tied down to business activity on a social media app. That feels like a ball and chain that my energy is not keen on lugging around. Does that mean I miss opportunities for business, follower growth and algorithm hacks? Yep. And I couldn't care less. You know why? Because my *energy* means more to me than all of that combined. Times a million.

It's time to reclaim your energetic wellbeing as the sacred, integral part of you that it is. That beautiful burning compass telling you your yes from no.

ACTIVITY: **Energetic hygiene**

With the above examples as inspo, think about how to start prioritising
energetic hygiene in your days.

_____

How can you weave them into your routines and rituals for living in
alignment?

Your takeaways:

- Identify the 'empath' behaviours you engage in versus the 'empathetic'. How can you identify less with the empath as an enabler to your people-pleasing ways?

- Get clear on what energetic depletion looks and *feels* like for you.

- Start to review your energetic-maintenance practices and commit to them as a non-negotiable part of your routines and rituals for living in alignment. These could be made up of rest, sleep, space, work/social/technological boundaries, body movement and vocal toning.

Stretch target:

- Watch 'The power of vulnerability' TED Talk by Brené Brown.

Next, we're diving deeper into that inner 'knowing' you are beginning to recognise. How do we listen to, trust in and – most importantly – live by our intuition?

CHAPTER 7

Intuition Made Me Do It

Imagine having a superpower that directly communicates to you what is a great or not-so-great decision, which friendships serve you versus those who don't, not to mention what the best dish to order off a menu is?

What if I told you that you don't have to imagine this at all? That the sixth sense isn't just reserved for M. Night Shyamalan movies? That we *all* have a superpower within us that is readily accessible but we just need to learn how to use it?

If there was one lesson – and one lesson only – I could ever share with the world, it would be how to listen to, trust and live by your intuition. In my opinion, your intuition is the not-so-secret key to unlocking your life's greatest potential, not to mention how to truly choose yourself in each and every moment. And, as you already know now, the key to begin this unlocking starts with your energetic maintenance – because our intuition communicates to us in the most subtle, gentle and often quiet ways. The first step to listening to her is to turn down all of the other 'noise' – the energy of others that you've been lugging around and even your own energetic baggage.

I find it really difficult to 'teach' intuition because – today – it's something I just 'do'. Like brushing my teeth, eating when I'm hungry and yes, getting in my naps when needed, living by and listening to my intuition is purely second nature. But it hasn't always been this way. I find that, for most of us, the journey to living deeply and intrinsically enmeshed with our intuition starts with our journey away from it.

The wisdom of not following your intuition

Take my initial rock-bottom moment, for example. Intuition was communicating to me loud and clear, on the daily, that it was time for me to leave that job and pursue something new. Now, at the time, I didn't recognise this 'voice' or 'inner knowing' as my intuition. If anything, I would have labelled it as an annoying little niggle that needed to be quiet, because didn't it know I had it all under control?! (Plot twist: I really didn't. And we *never* truly do. But more on control in a moment.)

Over a three-year period, intuition was gradually communicating to me that it was time for me to leave my job. It started as a gentle simmering – quiet enough to dismiss entirely, especially given my #busy lifestyle. The simmering grew to an annoying buzz – like a mosquito humming in your ear when you're trying to fall asleep. I became excellent at swatting it away, ignoring the seemingly 'random' thoughts of *Maybe I should just leave?* or *I don't think I'm very happy here* and even *This isn't the life meant for me*. The swatting away of intuitive niggles was effective mainly thanks to a very loud logical mind that would drown out said buzzing with facts. You already know the stories my mind was telling me. The voices of self-doubt and a low dosage of self-worth were running the show – reminding me I wasn't special enough to pursue anything different and that 'logically' I should stay in the 'secure' job with the decent salary and the nice colleagues.

The thing with intuition is that, when ignored, swatted or dismissed, it doesn't actually go anywhere. In fact, the voice/signs/niggles just become louder and more irritating the longer you ignore them. But rather than listen to them, instead we often partake in a screaming match internally between intuitive knowing and our matter-of-fact mind.

Mine, at this time, went a little like this:

Intuition: *Hollie, you've cried every Sunday for 18 months. I think it might be time to let this go.*

Mind: *Hollie, that is an absolutely ridiculous thought. How can you possibly leave when you have no idea what is next for you?*

Intuition: *But Hollie, you have that feeling. That knowing that it really will all be okay – because it will. Trust me. It will be okay.*

Mind: *How ridiculous. You can't possibly know for certain it will all be okay. Nope, it's far safer to stay put and in control.*

Intuition: *But Hollie, you're never really in control, even when you think you are. Wouldn't you rather take a risk and pursue a life that feels light and joyous?*

Mind: *I'll tell you what feels light and joyous. Stability. Not everyone loves their job, Hollie. You're no different.*

Now, in this instance, you know that my mind won for a solid chunk of time. I listened to her, but deep down I knew – I just *knew* – that there was more to life (thank you, Stacie Orrico). And what happened? I continued ignoring the niggles, even when my body was communicating very clear signs of energetic depletion (cue fatigue and burnout), even when it came at a cost to my mental health (which led to a much louder mind shouting over the top of any intuitive whisper) and even when it was clear my job was coming to an end whether I liked it or not.

This is the thing with our intuition … whether we listen to it or not, it is the true voice of reason. No matter what, the thing you intuitively 'know' *will* happen. And it is *so* much easier to accept it rather than fight it.

For you, perhaps you have an intuitive 'knowing' about a certain person, friendship or even lover in your life. Our mamas reading this will absolutely understand mother's intuition when it comes to your kiddies and just 'knowing' what they need in any given moment. Our intuition can communicate when something is right or wrong for us in career, living environment, even whether that online purchase is an aligned idea or not. And yes, just 'knowing' what's the best dish to order from a restaurant. It's a real thing, people! I meant it when I said every single decision I make today is intuitively guided. And I've never been more aligned (or less depleted!).

Communicating with our intuition

So, how does our intuition communicate with us? What does it sound like? Contrary to popular belief, our intuition isn't necessarily a drop-down montage-like visual of images playing out all of your life decisions and highlighting the yes versus the no. If only it were that simple, right? Our intuition is *far* more subtle than that, and because of this, it is so easy to dismiss.

There are a few things to consider with the way our intuition communicates to us. Firstly, it is a sense of just 'knowing'. Knowing something about yourself, someone else or a decision you've been faced with. Your intuition will communicate subtly to you. It will feel like clarity without even a single thought.

Now, what often happens here is that because we are so conditioned to worship the mind, we tend to outsource our intuitive 'knowings' to the mind, to start 'rationalising'. For instance, you might experience an intuitive knowing about a certain person you've recently connected with. You're not so sure about them, but you can't put your finger on how or why. It just feels 'off' to you. If you were to trust your intuition straight out, you would likely start to implement some boundaries with this person, without needing any further evidence to solidify your intuitive knowing. This is where trust comes in. (More on that in a moment.) However, if you're new to the knowing, your mind will likely tell you, 'Don't be silly, they've given you no reason not to trust them. Definitely go along to that next catch-up. You're overthinking things.' #ironic

When we ignore the niggles, we can get what I like to call a 'massive disruption' from the Universe/God/whatever higher power you believe in. In this instance, perhaps you continue to connect with the person in question while feeling 'off' about them, but dismiss the feels due to a lack of 'reason'. This can then lead to a number of challenging scenarios – maybe a misaligned friendship, a red-flag-waving love interest or even a phony business partner who runs off with all of your money (too dramatic?).

Wouldn't it have been easier if you just listened to the knowing in the first place? Now, just because you start to identify the 'knowings', it doesn't mean you will always listen to them. Heck, I was practising as an intuitive reader when the following example of ignoring my own intuition occurred.

When I first started out in my business, I wrote a list of the top ten brands I would love to collaborate with. 'Seemingly' out of nowhere, I received a call from one of those brands inviting me to collaborate with them on some workshops. Now, while logically this was a very exciting prospect (just that very morning I had written in my journal how I wanted to call in more speaking events!), intuitively, I had a sense that this wasn't going to be an aligned opportunity for me. During the phone call, while my mind was screaming 'Yes, yes, yes!' my body was retracting, feeling clammy and sending me all of the very blatant 'no' signs. So, I did what any intuitive person would do … I ignored it and listened to my mind. What proceeded to unfold were weeks of misaligned communication, feelings of being taken advantage of and lots of intuitive 'knowings' that this wasn't right for me. And yet, I continued to ignore these signs because logically, it was a 'smart' business move.

Let me tell you, friends, there is nothing *ever* smarter than listening to your intuition. On the first day of running one of these workshops, I woke up with a throbbing throat, aching limbs and all of the physical signs that were screaming *no* to the work I had said a very polite yes to. I believed that if I were to listen to my intuition at this point and say no to the brand in question, I would be letting them down and missing a good opportunity. So, yep, I chose the 'opportunity' and the brand over myself, over my own inner knowing and blatantly obvious physical cues that this truly was a no. Then I did it again the following week. And again the following week. It wasn't until I caught myself waking with such deep resentment, so familiar to my Sunday-itis in corporate land, that I had to snap myself out of it and recognise that yep, intuition was right – this was *not* an aligned decision for me, no matter how 'good' or even aligned it may have seemed on paper. So, after much more resistance, I chose me. I chose my intuition. Because she never leads me astray.

ACTIVITY: **Communicating with your intuition**

It's time to sit comfortably once more and close your eyes. This is a little exercise to guide you into what an intuitive 'yes' and 'no' feel like in your body. Remember, our intuition communicates to us through bodily signs, cues and sensations. If we get clear on these, we can start to act more from the feels rather than the thoughts.

Again, you can practise this by listening to the guided meditation here http://insighttimer.com/hollieazzopardi.

Find a comfortable seat or lay down, gently closing your eyes. First, take a big deep belly breath in, and let go on the exhale. Let's do that twice more together. Breathe in deeply through your nose – filling your belly – and exhale with a sigh through the mouth. One more. Beautiful. Now allow your breath to drop into its natural rhythm.

Take some time to connect with the breath, without any rush. Just allow the breath to settle your nervous system and calm the mind – remembering that if thoughts arise, they are part of the process. Simply observe without judgement. Notice the part of you that is separate to your thoughts.

I want you to recall a time in your life – perhaps a time coming up, or one from the past – where you said yes to something that deep down you wish you said no to. Perhaps this was a draining catch-up with a friend when you really wanted downtime, or maybe this was accepting poor behaviour from a loved one. Recall the experience – bring it to the front of your mind. Now, start to observe the sensations happening in your body. Where does this experience live? What sensations, feelings or emotions are moving through you right now? How do you feel?

Very gently deepening the breath, still keeping these feelings at the forefront of your mind, start to bring your awareness back to the space you're in. In your book or journal, jot down all of the feelings moving through you right now.

These are your intuitive 'no' sensations. The sensations that communicate to you when a decision, person or opportunity is not aligned.

Now, when you have these all captured, close your eyes and take a moment to gently stretch or shake to move this energy through your system. Start to connect with the breath once more – breathing in deeply through the nose, and out through the mouth. Allow your emotions, feelings and breath to settle. Use the exhale to release any tension or stagnant energy. Perhaps take an audible sigh or two to really move the energy through you.

Once you've settled your breath back down, allow your mind to call upon an experience you've had recently, or one on the horizon, that you feel deeply excited by. It feels aligned, inspiring and expansive. Notice here what is happening in your body. What is moving or shifting? What are the sensations, feelings or emotions? How do you feel?

Once you feel connected with these sensations, start to deepen the breath and very gradually bring yourself back into the space. In your book or journal, list all of the feelings and sensations running through your system right now.

These are your intuitive 'yes' sensations – the way your body communicates a 'yes' to you.

Trusting yourself

This is your intuitive starting point – you can use this exercise any time you feel there is too much 'head noise' about making a certain life decision, or even for the simplest of things, such as choosing where to order Uber Eats from or what clothes you want to wear. Rather than running away with the tabs in your mind shouting their loud options to you and justifying their reasons 'why' they know best, take a moment to sit, connect with the breath and *feel*. Once you turn down that noise, the decisions become far clearer.

However, there is a *key* component when it comes to actually listening to these voices of yes and no when they are intuitively guided: *trust*. Now, trust is a tricky one to teach, mainly because I find it only becomes stronger the more you practise it. Just like when you start deadlifting at the gym, you're not going to go straight to a 50-kilogram barbell. You're likely going to start with the technique before you even lift a single weight! The same goes for listening to and living by your intuition. Before we become masters, we've got to start with the technique.

A key piece of intuitive foundation is to start to trust ourselves more. This is where the challenge lies for most of us – especially those who have a tendency to trust everyone else before themselves. The hardest part is to trust in what *we* feel, above and beyond every other person with or without an opinion in our lives. And I don't know if you've noticed, but there are a *lot* of opinions flying around.

What I see happening *far* too much is an outsourcing of our intuitive knowing – our inner trust – to others. This happens in many contexts that have become quite normalised and thus super sneaky to catch. A simple vent to a bestie can have us on the receiving end of advice that goes directly against our inner knowing. If we have a tendency to trust our friends more than ourselves, this is an issue. A simple scroll of our social-media feeds can have us taking on the intuitive knowings of people we pedestal (let's stop doing that by the way) and telling ourselves, 'Well, I usually agree with everything they post, so this must be right for me too!'

In my years of sitting opposite hundreds of people from all walks of life, intuitively reading for them, one of the biggest pieces of feedback I receive is this: 'You just confirmed to me everything I already knew.' Boom. Therein lies the juice. *You already know.* And yet, because our trust is so shaky – mainly as we have been conditioned to *not* trust ourselves (the patriarchy, am I right?!) – we outsource. And, beautiful reader, your intuition is just not something that can be outsourced. Not even to an intuitive reader!

Acting on your intuition

So, how do we strengthen that muscle of trust? How do we feel ease within the discomfort of choosing to trust *our* knowing, perhaps over the louder, more entitled knowings of others? It starts with listening to *and acting on* your current intuitive knowings. It's not enough to hear them. You've got to *act* on them. Because in *these* moments, you're communicating to your intuition and saying, 'I trust you. Even though this is uncomfortable for me, I am listening to you.'

For some reason, I think people assume that to live intuitively is to live without a skerrick of discomfort. I'm sorry to break it to you, but this is a giant myth. To choose to listen to and trust your intuition will put you in some of the biggest periods of discomfort you will likely experience. This is what listening to and acting on my intuition has meant in my life:

- Leaving my 'stable' corporate role to pursue a life of self-employment without any clear direction as to how it would work out.
- Moving away from the only location I've ever lived – leaving all of my family and most of my friends behind – to start a new life.
- In the name of energetic alignment, saying no to opportunities that my former self would have jumped at.
- Going down some very twisty, random turns – all in the name of 'life lessons' – rather than a particular, clear-cut destination.

To live intuitively is one of the most rebellious acts you can partake in, especially in today's mass cultural worship of 'control'. Truth bomb: we are *never* in total control of our lives. Ever, ever. This is where you will be invited – time and time again – to trust in your 'knowing', even when it comes at a cost to your feelings associated with control.

Take it from my client Claire (name has been changed). Fuelled by a need to feel in control (hello, anxiety, we meet again), she knew there was more to life than her current job, but her mind just wouldn't let go of her need to know exactly how things would turn out. Underneath the noise of her mind, however, was a subtle knocking. An inner knowing that everything would be okay if she just trusted.

She started listening more and more to her intuitive knowings (through following the practices in this book) and now, not only has she been able to move on from hurt in past relationships causing her doubt in her own abilities, she has also been able to release negative habits and limiting beliefs keeping her stuck in needing to be in control. And now? She's transitioning away from her full-time role into part-time terrain while starting up her own dream freelance business! Because intuition told her to.

Now, this isn't to say we should dismiss the mind, logic or reason. Absolutely not – these components play a role too. We aren't going to leave a stable job and pursue a new path without some sort of financial support, for example. For me, this meant working in retail for 18 months while juggling freelance writing, promotional modelling and coaching sessions – yes, four jobs! Just like we aren't going to relocate without a home (or maybe van?) to move into. Logic and pragmatism play a role. But they aren't the *only* role. Your intuition is not a support act. She is a main character. It's time to shift her from the wings.

ACTIVITY: **My intuition tells me ...**

It's time to feel into the voice of your intuition. How does she speak to you? How is she different to the voice of your mind? *Today, intuition is telling me* ... is a favourite journal prompt of mine, and one I use regularly. That's it. Simply allow yourself to write down whatever lands (otherwise known as free writing).

Now, remember, this is where trust plays an integral role. The first few times you free write, you may doubt what comes up – notice how the mind interjects with thoughts such as 'this is stupid', 'I can't do this' or 'I'm doing it wrong'. Your intuition won't ever stop and think. She will simply flow. The other thing to note is that your intuition, much like the voice of your heart (no surprises that they're one and the same, right?), whispers gently. She speaks simply. Sometimes the words will run deep and long, but for the most part, they will be straightforward reminders and words of confirmation.

In this moment, what does my intuition have to tell me?

Now, once you have written this message, is there an action step you can take to *support* your intuitive 'niggle'? Remember, moments of self-doubt are likely to arise. If so, you might like to revisit your Five Whys practice and ask yourself: *why don't I trust my intuition?*

Whatever the case, committing to this practice as often as possible will allow you to turn up that little whisper of intuitive knowing so that she gets just as much airtime as, if not more than, the mind.

Intuition versus the mind

You've probably come to notice that there isn't any grand difference between the voices of your intuition and your mind. Because, most likely, they speak in the same voice!

I remember how groundbreaking it was for me when I realised this. Wait a second ... my intuition isn't a super psychic skill of clairvoyance or a voice in someone else's tone making it *super* clear for me to differentiate between it and the mind? For the most part, nope. Because while all of us may not have the gifts of clairvoyance (the ability to see psychically) or clairsentience (to feel, psychically), we *all* have an intuitive ability. Some have just fine-tuned theirs more than others. They've lifted the weights for longer. They trust in the voice more. That is the only major difference.

So, let's look at some exercises we can do to strengthen this not-so-little muscle of ours, shall we?

My go-to practices for strengthening intuition

- *Meditation*

  Meditation quietens the mind and creates space for introspection, which are key skills for listening to your intuition. Now, for many of us (myself included), our resistance to meditating lies in our misunderstanding of it. Meditation is *not* about turning off your thoughts or even sitting comfortably every time – far from it. *But*, committing to regular meditation *does* allow you to become more comfortable with feelings of discomfort, silence and even identifying times when the mind is noisier than others. There are a multitude of guided meditation apps for beginners. However, if you're looking to deepen your practice, seeking out a teacher is something to consider. When I first learned to practise Vedic meditation, my teacher was receiving incredibly random calls from me asking if the heightened intuitive, and even psychic, experiences I was having in my meditations were 'normal'. It can open up levels of awareness that are impossible to access in any other way.

- *Journalling*

  No surprises that meditation, followed by journalling, are my key practices not just for living in alignment but also for paving the way for writing (including this book!). Journalling allows me to process any head noise, clear the cobwebs of my mind and access my intuition. There are no right or wrong ways to journal – you can't high-achieve this! Some days, I'll simply dump onto the page everything that is taking up mental space (like taking a feather duster to the cobwebs), because it clears my mind and creates perspective when I see what I've written. Other times, I'll reflect on any thoughts that have arisen in my meditation practice. Sometimes, I'll use a journalling prompt – like the intuition one earlier! This is where the simple act of trust can be strengthened by asking yourself: What do I *feel* like writing about today?

- *Signs and synchronicities*
  If I received a dollar for every DM, message and call from
  friends, family and strangers alike asking me what seeing 11:11
  all the time meant, your gal would be *very* wealthy. We are
  constantly being fed signs and 'coincidences' on the daily. Now,
  your relationship with faith is a very personal part of the intuitive
  journey. Perhaps you are religious, and your relationship with
  faith is intrinsically linked to your religious beliefs. Maybe
  you connect more with the Universe and ascended masters.
  Or maybe you see number patterns and call them your 'angel
  numbers' as a way to connect with your guardian angels.
  Whatever the case, in my opinion, there is no such thing as
  coincidence. Synchronicities, signs and patterns are all indicators
  that you are on the right path. Whenever you are doubting
  a decision or the voice of your intuition, ask for a sign. My
  signs have taken the form of angel numbers, lady beetles, red
  dragonflies and even songs. Your signs are for *you* to decipher.
  How do they make *you* feel? And rather than sliding into
  someone else's DMs to determine what they mean to *them*
  (hello, intuitive outsourcing!), drop in deeper and ask yourself,
  what do they mean to *me*?

- *Oracle cards*
  It would be remiss of me to write about intuitive practices
  without mentioning all of the tools we have at our disposal to
  strengthen our inner knowing. The best place to start is to work
  with a deck of oracle cards. Now, this may not be for everyone,
  but for me, when I first started to listen to my intuition more,
  the wisdom of these cards helped support me in trusting what
  I already knew to be 'truth'. When it comes to picking a deck,
  again, don't outsource this question to someone you admire.
  Avoid copying what you see someone else using. This is a very
  beautiful opportunity to trust what you are being *drawn* to – what
  deck is calling you? What *feels* like an intuitive yes when you hold
  it in your hands? The same goes for those of you choosing to
  work with crystals or essential oils (other lovely supportive tools

to strengthen your relationship with your intuition). What feels good for *you*? Do that. Choose that.

- **Trust!**

    I know I've already banged on about this, but consider this the final bold, underlined, exclamation-marked emphasis point. Your intuition will only strengthen insofar as your ability to act on and trust in it. It really is that simple (although not always simple in practice, I know!).

When I started working with Laura (name has been changed), it was clear she had a natural connection with her intuition. However, what was lacking were regular practices to help her listen to, and strengthen, her intuitive 'muscle'. Self-doubt was running the show.

Through engaging in the above regular practices, Laura was able to shift her self-described 'daily negative mindset fuelled by what-ifs' to a state of deep trust that everything is unfolding as it is meant to. This has helped her navigate life's most challenging experiences – from financial sticking points to a miscarriage – because her entire outlook on life changed. Not only this, but Laura has been able to show up for her two young children by teaching them to use these tools as well, cultivating a shift in their own mini mindsets for their future.

ACTIVITY: **Your intuitive practices**

How are you going to start strengthening your intuitive muscles and work these practices into your alignment rituals?

_____

Capture below the practices that are calling you and, alongside each practice, add an *action* step to put the wheels in motion:

The reason our intuition is a key component in putting ourselves first is that our intuition is the voice of alignment – every time. When listening to her, even when the road gets twisty, she is *always* guiding us with our best interest at heart towards the people, moments, lessons and everything in between for our highest good.

When you live intuitively, you are far less inclined to place anyone else's perspective above your own. You can have constructive conversations, absolutely, but underneath it all is a very deep knowing and trust that *you* have your back, before anyone else does. Truly, there is nothing more liberating than that.

CHAPTER 7 **SUMMARY**

Your takeaways:

- Start to practise the 'intuitive knowing meditation' – get super clear on what yes and no *feel* like in your body. Start to act from this intuitive place as often as feels comfortable (or even slightly uncomfortable …).

- Begin to regularly use the 'what does intuition want me to know?' journalling prompt. Start to become aware of the voice of intuition, and how subtle the differences are between that and the voice of your mind.

- Plan your intuition-strengthening practices – perhaps starting a regular meditation or journalling practice, or maybe keeping an eye on signs and synchronicities. Consider a deck of oracle cards if that feels aligned for you.

Stretch target:

- Now that you are clear on the voice of intuition, how can you take ongoing *action* as an act of trust?

Look at you go! Living the aligned life, cultivating practices that scream 'this gal knows her worth' and making the sometimes-difficult decisions in finally putting yourself first. What an #inspo you are – the hard work is well and truly done! Or, is it?

Because here's the thing ... we can do *all* of the work in the world when it comes to living in alignment and finally choosing ourselves, but what's the easiest way to be derailed from these practices? The voices, opinions and connections we have with others – be it our loved ones, friends, family and even strangers on the internet. It's time to talk connection.

Know Thy People

CHAPTER 8

Connection and Friendships

My first-ever friend is still my best friend today. In what can only be described as a wholesome Hollywood-esque moment, two next-door neighbours went door knocking selling cookies for a local fundraiser and realised that they were part of the same parents' group. Said neighbours became best friends and raised their daughters together. Those daughters happen to be me and my best friend, Leah. (Shout out to Mama Kaye and Mama Jen for making it happen!)

Leah is the friend I mentioned earlier – the one I share voice note gratitudes with every single day. And in our 31 years of friendship (keep in mind, I'm only 32!), we've experienced it all: we started our first day of school together, we got our first periods within a day of each other, we moved out of home for the first time together and we have travelled the world side-by-side. She was a bridesmaid at my wedding, while I was present via many erratic texts when she went into labour with her firstborn, Ziggy.

A friendship like ours is rare. We speak our own language (literally, we could rewrite the dictionary with the words we've made up), we get mistaken for sisters and even our first visit to a psychic more than ten years ago had it confirmed: 'You two are the definition of soul sisters. Your souls have actually been sisters in other lives.' My wish is for everyone to have a friendship like I do with Leah. One where there is zero pressure, where you can live a plane trip away and still connect daily, where you can grow and change through all of life's challenges and still stand together.

But I also know that a friendship like this is hard to come by. If, while reading this, you are reflecting on your own special friend(s), I invite you to take a moment to drop into deep gratitude for that connection. Maybe pick up the phone and remind them how much they mean to you. Because, not only is a friendship like this rare, it is the deep desire of so many. And it is not lost on me how lucky I am to have it.

A question I am asked regularly – one of the most frequent questions I am asked, actually – is this: how do I call in like-minded connections? Or, to put it in layman's terms: where the friends at?

Your friendship values

I've always been good at making friends. I think it's because I'm so fuelled to make everyone feel comfortable, teamed with my natural tendency to ask all of the questions (#journalist), and I've been told my energy leaves people feeling good about themselves, which is a bonus.

My mum also raised me to be kind to every person I cross paths with, which is very beautiful, but also fed the people pleaser in me. I thought that meant I had to be friends with every person who wanted to be friends with me, which doesn't necessarily sound like an issue on the surface, but let's scratch a little deeper …

Something I have only recently been navigating is my very specific set of friendship values, and how important they are when choosing to connect with others. Because connection really is that – a choice. A choice in where we direct our time, energy and words. And we know by now that all of this truly matters when it comes to living in alignment.

It's taken me relocating out of the city I was born and raised in – leaving most of my dearest loved ones behind – to force me to take massive stock of my friendships and how they serve me. Because I've always been surrounded by lovely people, I've never thought it was necessary to evaluate whether said lovely people actually add value to my life or not. And I know reading that sounds incredibly harsh – trust me, this has been a very confronting part of the process – but again, mainly confronting for the people pleaser in me.

The people pleaser in me wants to be friends with anyone and everyone, regardless of the value they bring me, or I them, because I can't be bothered with conflict and I don't want to hurt anyone's feelings. The people pleaser in me thinks I *should* be friends with everyone, discrediting whether I actually want to be friends with everyone or not. The people pleaser in me tells me I have the space in my calendar for the catch-up, so obviously I should say yes to the catch-up request. The people pleaser in me tells me it's the kind, good and 'right' thing to meet up with the person who has reached out on social media for in-person time, even though I have incredibly limited time for myself and my husband, let alone cultivating a new connection. Do we see the patterns here?

It's time to get clear on what your people pleaser is telling you about the friendships you have, or *should have*, in your life.

ACTIVITY: **The people pleaser in me ...**

In reflecting on how you are showing up in your friendships right now – be that the lifelong ones or the newbies – start to list all of the ways the people pleaser in you is running the show.

The people pleaser in me is ...

Now that you are clear on these inner workings, let's re-establish what we truly desire in our friendships and what we do not.

For example, let's look at my belief: *The people pleaser in me thinks I should be friends with everyone, discounting whether I actually want to be friends with everyone, or not ...*

My ideal reframe would be something like this: *I choose to be friends with people who align with my values and leave me feeling inspired, supported and connected. I do not place any pressure on myself to be friends with someone just because they want to be friends with me.*

Do we see the difference?

Here is another example: *The people pleaser in me tells me I have the space in my calendar for the catch-up, so obviously I should say yes.*

My ideal reframe would be along the lines of this: *Space in my calendar is sacred and reserved for myself first, then for people I genuinely look forward to connecting with. I only say yes to catch-ups that light me up.*

It's your turn! Let's get clear on some of your reframes:

Meaningful friendships

I was sitting in a deep kinesiology session with my kinesiologist Zoe Bosco (who is also one of my good friends) last year, and the subject of friendships came up. We had never touched on it before and when it arose, I almost dismissed Zoe, telling her I was surrounded by wonderful friends, I had so many it was hard to keep up with them all and I didn't need any help in that arena (oh the naivety!).

I'm sure Zoe humoured me briefly but, like any good energy practitioner, she also invited me to look a little deeper. I will never forget that session – she asked me, 'Hollie, what makes a good friend?' My response was quick – I didn't even have to pause to think: 'Well, obviously a good friend is someone who is there for you when you need them, and offers you support. I know I'm a good friend because I'm always there to help my friends when they need me.' 'Mmhmm. And outside of when they need your support, what makes a good friend?' she asked. I was stuck. Trumped. Honestly, I couldn't answer it. We went around and around in circles as I kept rephrasing what a 'good friend' meant to me – I could literally only define friendship through the lens of offering help and support when needed. And this was how I was showing up in many of my friendships. The fixer. The helper. The support giver. And yet, when I needed the same? There were moments I felt I wasn't receiving it (mostly because I wouldn't ask).

This discussion planted a tiny seed that has since sprouted as I've relocated and been put in a position to cultivate new friendships, while maintaining the old from a distance. What makes a friendship a friendship? I realise now that my friendship lens was so fiercely adjusted to 'be of service' mode that I was missing all of the other beautiful, enriching and valuable components true connection can bring. Let's take a look at yours …

ACTIVITY: **My friendship story**

Take a moment to reflect on your definition of friendship. What does it mean to be a good friend? How do you show up in this way in your friendships?

I call someone a friend when …

My answer would look a little like this:

> I call someone a friend when I know I can pick up the phone and have a conversation about anything without a filter (and that's saying a lot, because I hate phone calls. If I want to call someone – they really are a friend!). A friend, to me, is someone I can show up to without any masks, and who expects nothing from me other than to be my true self. There is no judgement, gossip or criticism and instead pure love, support and respect – even if we have differing views or opinions. I can call someone a friend when I feel safe to share my truths with them and when it can go for weeks or even months without talking – but when we do, it's as if nothing has changed. I enjoy their company, time doesn't exist in their presence and while we may not have all of the same values, above all, we are there for one another when we need support and love.

So, while yes, my clear value of giving and receiving support is still woven into my friendship story, there is also so much more to it. Friendship to me is a mutual exchange of aligned values. Respect of each other's beliefs and journeys. Celebrating each other's successes and milestones. Freedom to be who we truly are – not the people-pleasing version of who we *think* we should be. And I've only realised this recently in experiencing a few tension points in connections pointing to what I truly value (and what I do not).

Expectations in friendships

When I was in my first trimester of pregnancy (timed nicely with when I started to write this book), I felt incredibly lonely. Now, loneliness is a funny thing. People presume being alone and loneliness are the same, however in my experience, they are far from it. Loneliness doesn't care if you're happily married, growing a child or surrounded by people who want to catch up with you. Loneliness is a feeling that takes over when we feel isolated, separated or, for me in this particular experience, forgotten.

Now, it's not lost on me that there were a multitude of hormones rushing through my body that were adding to and exacerbating these feelings. Also, the first trimester is one of those tough moments where not everyone is fully aware of what you are navigating and, even if they are, social catch-ups are incredibly difficult when you literally cannot leave the couch because you are so unwell.

For three months, I felt lonely, depressed and, to be frank, let down by some of my friends. Because I had absolutely minimal to offer as a friend – by way of energy or ability to really laugh, play or be my usual vibrant self – I felt that that I wasn't offering anything of value in the 'friendship stakes', so the calls and check-ins were minimal, the visits verging on non-existent and I was left feeling very sorry for myself.

Now, this isn't actually my friends' fault. They're not mind-readers, and I had relocated across the state which made it very difficult for them to pop in. But what this experience did teach me is, in the context of our friendships, there is a thin line that dances between the expectations we place on others and our values.

In fact, I wrote about this exact inner conflict I was navigating only a month ago in my journal:

> I'm dancing with the fine line of compassion and intolerance. Where do you no longer tolerate poor behaviour from someone, but still hold them in compassion? I think it comes down to understanding but still prioritising yourself and your values. It's a very fine line, but one I need to tread lightly now as I create a re-prioritisation of what (and who) deserves my time, energy and love.

Put simply, this is about exploring where we are placing unfair expectations on the people we love (to be a mind-reader, to check in without us asking, etc.) and where our friendship values are simply not aligning.

This recent experience felt incredibly familiar to me, as I found myself reflecting on the last time I had felt 'forgotten' by friends. And, no surprises, it took me right back to my first rock bottom when my health was near non-existent, and – low and behold – I couldn't leave the couch, let alone attend birthday gatherings or play my usual friendship role of 'planner of the catch-ups'. At that time, I had two very clear friendship categories: the ones who showed up for me, kept me company while I was couch-bound, checked in regularly with calls and messages and 'carried the friendship load', so to speak, and the friendships that dissipated when I was no longer there to fuel them.

While confronting at the time, this experience taught me that there were friendships I was holding far more closely to my heart than perhaps the people in question were holding to theirs. I was challenged by my therapist at the time to start to 'drop the ball' a little with these friendships – not in any blatant ways, just allowing myself to no longer be the 'planner', the one who always checks in, the load carrier. Read: the good girl, the people pleaser. What happened? A number of friendships completely slipped away. They disappeared because there was no even value exchange when it came to time or energy.

The ebb and flow of friendships

When it comes to aligning our friendships, it's a natural part of life that, yes, some will be forever (what a gift!) but, just as likely, some will slip away. Trent and I often marvel at our wedding guest list from only three years ago – three years! – and how radically different it would look today. I was part of a wedding party for a friend who I haven't spoken to, let alone seen, in close to five years. And while, yes, nostalgia can come creeping in from time to time, for the most part, I've made peace with the fact that there is real validity in that Instagrammable quote from Brian A 'Drew' Chalker's famous poem: 'People come into your life for a reason, a season or a lifetime.'

Rather than finding sadness in the fact that every person you hold dear to you today may not be who you hold dear in a year's or a decade's time, can you find the lessons, gifts and even liberation in allowing people to come and go – to move through your life and either grow and change as you do, or naturally shift away – without judgement, conflict or regret?

ACTIVITY: **Your reasons, seasons and lifetimes**

It's time to get some closure. And no, we're not randomly calling old numbers that shouldn't be taking up space in our contacts anymore. We're going to gift ourselves a little exhale – recognising that while some friendships have drifted or ended, perhaps they left a little gift behind.

First, let's reflect on all of the friendships in your life – past or present – that you believe were gifted for a *reason*. You might like to define reason in this case as a lesson, a particular moment you needed them or something different.

My reasons:

Now, let's look at your seasons. Like that friend of yours from uni who liked to read the same trashy mags as you in the back of your cultural studies tutorial or the one you used to party hard with back in your heyday. They were great for the season in your life they served, however, now that it's no longer spring, it's time for some shedding.

My seasons:

Finally, let's contemplate your lifetimes. These are your Leah equivalents, yes, but also more than that – the people you feel deeply connected to at a soul level. For example, while our wedding guest list would absolutely be different today, our bridal party would remain the same because it was made up of our lifetime people. Who are yours?

My lifetimes:

Now, you will likely find in doing this exercise that there are friends who don't fall into any of these categories – that's normal! That new friend of yours could end up being the ultimate lifetimer, or maybe more a season in your life. It's hard to say sometimes, and that's perfectly okay. What matters here is that we start recognising that, unlike our 12-year-old selves would like to believe – seeing every person you have a friendly relationship with as a BFFL just isn't realistic. Friendships drifting, moulding, changing and forming are normal. And guess what? Conflict needn't be a big part of it a lot of the time.

Self-inquiry in friendships

I see it time and time again in people-pleasing behaviours. Holding on tightly to a friendship that may have been a reason or a season, hoping beyond hope that it will shift into lifetime territory, because the thought of releasing said friendship causes overwhelm or stress. It challenges the pleaser in you to assert boundaries, but in doing this over time, it can also lend itself to acceptance of poor behaviour. I was exploring this in my journal entry earlier. When we love someone and appreciate having them in our lives, it can be incredibly challenging to recognise behaviours that perhaps don't align with our values or are even a complete overstep of our boundaries. But, again, when we haven't asserted any boundaries in the first place, this isn't actually on the friend in question.

There is a big belief in personal-development arenas that expectations lead to disappointment. That if you place expectations on a certain relationship – be it friendship, familial, romantic or otherwise – you will almost always be met with disappointment in some form. While, yes, this is true, I offer up the question: why are we avoiding disappointment? In fact, when it comes to getting super clear on the connections you value versus the ones that no longer align, disappointment is a brilliant identifier of a relationship needing a closer look. I challenge the idea that no expectations is the goal here because, let's be real, surely there are some non-negotiable behaviours that you would expect as a minimum from your loved ones?

My expectations in a relationship of any kind are to be treated with kindness, fairness and respect, and to be offered support when needed (there's that value of mine again!).

When these expectations aren't present (for example, the lack of support from some of my friends in my early stages of pregnancy), it points to disappointment, followed by a need for me to enquire about the role I played in this dynamic. As the saying goes, for every finger you point, there are three pointing back at you. This basically means that, while my disappointment in these instances is directly linked to behaviours of loved ones in my life, I also played a role in allowing these behaviours to occur. (Hello, people pleaser.)

For example, I could have made it clearer to some of my friends just how much I was struggling in the first trimester. Maybe sharing I felt lonely wasn't enough? Maybe I needed to spell out clearly, 'I really need your support right now.' Also, my past patterns in friendships have been to let my boundaries slide because I'm an expert conflict avoider. Maybe you are too? So, with this in mind – knowing that we train people with what is acceptable or not in our interactions with them – of course, over time, behaviours like belittling or co-dependency can become the norm … Because we allow it.

Notice how this level of self-enquiry starts to highlight the role *we* play in challenging friendship dynamics? Once we're clear on our *own* role, we can create real change. We can have the conversation asserting the new boundaries (more on that in Chapter 9). I've been known to, as of only this year, say very clearly: 'Right now, you are crossing a boundary of mine and I would appreciate it if you would stop.' This isn't always received well, however it is *always* an opportunity for an open discussion on my own boundaries and the person's in question. We can get clearer in our communication of certain expectations. For example, saying something like: 'I was really struggling and perhaps I didn't make that clear enough to you. I understand you have your own stuff going on and I never want to be a burden, but at that time I really would have appreciated some support.' We can even start to create loving distance in certain dynamics, particularly the instances where our minimal expectations are no longer being met and boundaries are continually being crossed. Loving distance can simply look like less availability, reliance or contact with the person in question.

ACTIVITY: **My expectations and blind spots**

Consider this your giant permission slip to *expect*. Yep, I'm going there. Let's stop the shame around placing minimal expectations on the behaviours that create alignment in our friendships.

What are my friendship expectations?

Now that you are clear on these, you might like to ask yourself:
Where does my disappointment in certain connections in my life right now allow me an opportunity for self-enquiry? What role have I played in the creation of this disappointment?

With this level of self-awareness now, you might like to also ask yourself:

How can I start to take action to create some changes in the ways I am allowing misaligned behaviour in these friendships?

Honouring your values in friendships

Now, here's where we get to the nitty-gritty. Because it's one thing to highlight others' behaviours that do not align and take action accordingly, but it's another thing to recognise that *we* are the misaligned friend in question. It's the nature of relating to people. It's also just a fact of life that there will be people we 'get' and vibe with more than others. But it's so important that we recognise our *own* friendship growth areas so that we're not sitting in victim land or wallowing in 'woe is me' territory.

For every friendship strength you hold, there is likely an area for growth. For example, some of my friendship strengths are:
- Offering help, advice and support when needed (I mean, it's very apparent this is one of my key friendship values by now, right?).
- Generosity – I love to give gifts, shower friends in surprises (just this week we sent a cheese board to friends of ours in lockdown 'just because') and I'm *big* on the Instagram Story birthday montage.
- No judgement – I'm a clean slate when it comes to my friends' views, opinions and life experiences. I do not judge, even when our views differ. I'm a safe space for my friends.

Here are my growth areas, which complement those strengths:
- I can offer unsolicited advice at times and verge on 'I told you so' territory when a friend just needs me to listen.
- Sometimes, I expect people to match my generosity. I don't give to receive, but when someone forgets my birthday or the generosity doesn't match up, it really challenges me.
- Because I hold space for many of my friends, I don't often allow them to hold me. It's rare for me to admit to friends when I need help, but how can I expect them to support me when I haven't asked for it?

This is where our friendship values become more and more apparent. And sometimes, it's just a matter of getting clear on these and noticing where they match up and where they do not.

In reviewing my values only this year, I've recognised that some friendships meet every value of mine (the lifetimes), some meet a portion, but perhaps not all, and some don't meet any of them. This is no criticism of any of the people in question, because all of our values differ (and also change, as we change). But what this does start to highlight is where we place our friendship priorities. Who gets VIP access based on our levels of alignment and who needs a little re-jigging?

Because, beautiful reader, I'm sorry to break it to you, but you *cannot* be every single person's bestie. I don't think you even want to, though, am I right? Connection is about *quality* over *quantity*. Unfortunately, our views on 'popularity' would have it perceived the other way – the more friends in your life, the better. I've come to learn that the more *key, quality* and *aligned* people you have in your circle, the more fulfilled you will feel. You'll also feel less pressured, resentful and exhausted.

ACTIVITY: **Your friendship values**

It's time to get clear on those values in friendships you hold dearly.

To start, let's have a look at your strengths in your friendships:

Look at you! Some beautiful qualities there. Now, with those in mind, can you start to notice where your growth areas might be?

In doing these activities, it's likely that your friendship values are very apparent. Remember, with our values – or in this book at least – there can be as many or as little as you like. Have them as a word, a feeling, a sentence – mix it up. Also, don't forget, these *will* change over time.

For example, right now in this stage of my life, my friendship values are:

- **Support**
  As my life drastically changes in the lead-up to birthing my little girl and this book, at the same time (#highachiever), I really value the friends who are reaching out and offering me support with check-ins, pep talks and yep, even gift hampers and flower deliveries (I really do have some great friends!).

- **Independence**
  This might sound like a funny one, but I've come to realise I am the type of friend who thrives in space and suffocates in co-dependency. I love friendships right now where we can go days, weeks, sometimes even months, without checking in, because #life but, when we do, it's like nothing has changed. There's no pressure. (One of my favourite things my friends and I say to each other is, 'Never apologise for a delay in reply, that's life!')

- **Respect**
  It is important to show respect for others' viewpoints, perspectives and differences. I'm writing this as our collective macro world experiences a mass divide when it comes to personal perspectives on the state of the world. I value friendships where we don't judge each other for our points of view or life experiences.

- **Love and kindness**

  If you're unkind, critical, judgemental or just plain mean, I'm not interested. Life is way too short to accept behaviour less than love, and I've come a long way in no longer allowing anything less in my life.

Your turn!

My friendship values right now are:

Now that you are clear on your friendship values, strengths and areas for growth, perhaps there are certain actions to take with connections in your life that no longer serve you. Remember, this needn't look like conflict or animosity. It can simply take the form of:

- Asserting new boundaries
- Clear communication
- Creating loving distance

Calling in like-minded connections

Now that you have navigated the *current* connections in your space, how the heck do you call in new ones? I have actually never met one of my most aligned friends right now in person. In fact, we only started chatting – via Instagram of all places – a year ago. When I first stumbled across Britt's profile, I was taken by her way with words. The topics she wrote about, her conversational and up-front approach in her Stories and the fact that she was pregnant with a little girl too – a fire sign, #twins! – was enough to catch my attention. She got me, I got her and we didn't even know each other yet.

Our online friendship was a slow burn. When Britt slid into my DMs, the encounter was brief. Over the next few months, our interactions were a few reactions to her Stories on my part (smooth Hollie. Smooth). Before long, the reactions and 'me toos!' turned into lengthy messages and voice notes, and has since evolved into a beautiful long-distance friendship including birthday flower deliveries and invitations to one another's baby blessingways. And I repeat, we have never met in person before. I told you, I'm an expert friend maker.

The biggest piece of advice I can give for calling in like-minded connections is to *connect* with like-minded people. Literally. It's that simple. How are you going about your days cultivating new connections? It's not enough to simply like or follow people online, waiting for the coffee catch-up invitations to land in your Instagram DMs. How are you championing people? Supporting their work? Sharing their stuff? Attending their events or workshops? Buying their art?

Never underestimate the impact of a loving comment in someone's inbox (or mailbox, if we're going old school!) or a thoughtful comment online (not just an emoji, I'm talking honest, considered conversation). But, remember, Instagram is not a love language. Where are you taking connection *off* social platforms, too?

What rooms are you entering with like-minded people? Are you taking courses led by people you admire, knowing that their community is likely also the community for you? In running my signature online program for four years now, with six intakes, I've found that the *biggest* gift of the program is the level of connection made with the women in the community. *That* is the gift – being seen, heard and held by like-minded people on the same path as you. But you *must* get in the room (or on the screen). Remember, nothing changes if nothing changes.

I have lost count of the number of friendships I have made on Instagram. No kidding. For all of its challenges and frustrations (take it from the gal who has it deleted from her phone as she writes this), when used with consideration, it is a wonderful platform for connecting with like-minded people. And no, this doesn't mean every DM you slide into will end up with a bestie on the other side of the country. However, it does mean you are getting closer to cultivating those connections. A simple, 'I just want you to know how much I appreciate what you do,' can really make the difference between an online acquaintance and a friend.

I was reflecting recently on my journalling from five years ago about who in the health and wellness industry I admired the most. Alongside Oprah sat two beautiful women who I am so grateful to call my friends today (shout out to Rachel MacDonald and Tara Bliss). I wrote their names in my journal because I admired their energy and their work and one day hoped to carve out a life like them. They didn't know me, but I knew them. I loved their work and made it clear to them. Now, they're in my Voxer contacts and close friends lists and are only a message away if I need them.

Making yourself vulnerable enough to tell people that you admire them can be the beginning of a friendship. Not in a super-clingy 'I think we could be best friends!' way, though. I've lost count of how many times I've received a message like that and, while well intentioned, it may come across as a little boundary overstep.

It's all about your *genuine*, authentic voice. Being the person you are innately here to be. Not the person you *think* other people will accept or like more (this is where we start to change the people-pleasing game).

Again, need I remind you that people-pleasing tendencies in friendships can be a form of manipulation? We are literally (and unintentionally for the most part) manipulating people's perspectives of us – to be accepted – versus just showing up as who we really are. I think that's one of the things that sets me up for beautiful connections – that I'm always myself when I first meet people. Remember, your energy doesn't lie. Be *you*. And watch who is drawn into your space due to your innate magnetism, and who falls away.

ACTIVITY: **I am who I am**

It's time to claim it! What makes you, you? The quirks, idiosyncrasies, sense of humour? The parts of you that perhaps in the past you may have 'toned down' to be more palatable or acceptable to others?

_____

It's time for a reclamation – what are your unique skills, gifts and personality traits? List them all below (and ask a friend for help if you get stuck!).

There you have it! When you're next sliding into a DM, attending a course or workshop, or taking a coastal stroll – how can you embody more of the _you_ listed above?

Ways to connect IRL

Now, it's not all about the Instagram DM slide. Remember, we were connecting with one another _long_ before social media was a thing (who would have thought?!). Some ways I have cultivated beautiful connections in my life that do not involve a screen include:
- Going to gatherings, celebrations and dinners of friends-of-friends. Perhaps I would consider them more of an acquaintance

than a close friend; however, knowing there will be a table of new people to meet – while daunting – is an opportunity to practise conversing with new people. Be the one to ask the questions, and really listen to the answers. Get curious. Pay attention to what your energy is doing while in the presence of new people – are they an energetic yes, or a no? Do you contract or expand in their presence? Spend more time with those who are a yes! Trust what the vibes are telling you. (And then follow up with an Insta DM slide if you're really feeling it!)

- Remembering people's names and *using* them in conversation. Not to be underestimated, people! Call your barista, chiropractor and beautician by their names! This simple act illustrates that a) you care and b) you're connecting with them on a more personal level.
- Smiling! Smile at strangers, at your next waiter or waitress, at the person who seems familiar to you but you just can't place them. Truly, flirting need not be reserved for matters of romance! A smile, eye contact, even a light tap on the arm in agreeance with someone are all ways to connect with someone on a deeper level. It also makes people feel comfortable in your presence, and who doesn't want to spend time with someone who makes it safe to be themselves?
- Doing the course, working with the person I look up to, putting myself in spaces where it is guaranteed the attendees will be like-minded. Some of my closest friends today started out as my naturopath, business coach, meditation teacher and even women whose workshops and events I attended – front row, fan-girl flag waving wildly, lining up to get my book signed.

There are a multitude of ways to call in connections, but the key is that *you* must do the calling. This doesn't mean it will feel effortless and easy all the time, and it also doesn't mean every one of your smiles will be met with one in return. But remember, every no or roadblock is getting you closer to a yes – to your people. And the more ways you are living a life that is in truest alignment to *you* and what *you* value, the more naturally these connections will fall into (and away from) your life.

Your takeaways:

- Get clear on what the people pleaser in you is telling you about friendships.

- Create a reframe of these supporting your new approach to cultivating connections that serve you.

- Write your friendship story – what makes a friend to you?

- List the friends that make up your *reasons, seasons* and *lifetimes*.

- Identify your friendship expectations and blind spots.

- Get clear on your friendship strengths, growth areas and values.

- Celebrate what makes *you* uniquely you and start to show up as that version more and more.

Stretch targets:

- Take some action based on the earlier exercises – do any connections need some boundaries asserted? Maybe a conversation?

- Start to show up in rooms, platforms and DMs of people you align with being your fullest, most authentic self.

Next, we're going to dive into the work that most people pleasers will run right away from. I've saved the best for last. Yep, it's time to talk boundaries. After years – perhaps even your entire life – running from boundaries, for whatever reason (fear of conflict, wanting to be loved or even deep-seated trauma responses from your childhood), it's time to reclaim them as an act of liberation – for yourself and your loved ones.

CHAPTER 9

Boundaries

When I was a ten-year-old in Year 5 at school, my peers gave me one of my very first nicknames. I remember it clearly – I was labelled the 'goody-goody'. It was such an identifier put upon me (mostly by the boys in my class) that I even remember using the phrase as my password for my first-ever email address (jolly-hollie, for those of you curious. Give me a break – I was ten).

It didn't really sting and, as far as juvenile nicknames went, I knew it could have been worse. I also knew I *was* the good girl – I never stepped a foot wrong, my teachers loved me and I excelled in my studies. Being good activated an innate sense of worth within me. It was how I saw myself in the world. But, even bigger than that, it was how I felt *safe* in the world. To be good meant recognition. It meant praise and validation. It meant achievement. It meant love.

I was okay with being the goody-goody because that was the way I was raised. Perhaps it came with being the eldest child, or maybe the outcome of a fairly tumultuous family life where I decided to play the role of peacekeeper and, often, parent to my younger siblings.

All I know is that this innate good-girl complex was how I kept safe. I rarely, if ever, stepped a foot wrong – at home or at school. If I ever *was* to get in trouble, the guilt of doing something wrong was debilitating. I would carry it with me for days and it was the source of many a panic attack. So, I avoided being 'bad' and I played by the rules because I believed the rules were there to protect me.

Perhaps you can relate to this in your own way. Maybe you're reading this and identifying as the 'good' daughter. The 'good' student. The 'good' friend. The 'good' mum.

Being the 'good' girl

The weight of the word 'good' stems right back to when we were babies fresh out of the womb. Phrases such as, 'Is she a good girl?' and 'What a good boy sleeping well for Mum and Dad!', and even using 'good' as a descriptor to brush aside pain, emotion or frustration points we experienced as a child (when we are our most impressionable), have a deeply ingrained effect on our psyche. We start to associate 'good' with reward, praise and being loveable and accepted by others.

The opposite of good? Bad. And being 'bad' – while subjective – has also been ingrained in us in a similar way growing up. We are deemed 'bad' when we turn our heads when offered a kiss from a family member – being encouraged to be 'polite' rather than 'rude', and accept the physical affection even when we really don't want it. 'That's a good girl.' Through mirroring our own parents' definitions of what is good and bad, we start to embody behaviours that prioritise the wellbeing of others – their feelings, values and expectations – over our own. Because being good = being loved. And being bad = guilt.

It was only in my late twenties that I started to slowly break up with the good-girl complex I'd been carting along my entire life. Expectations placed on me from family members – minute as they may seem, like always answering a phone call even if I didn't have the energy, time or space to – started to fall away. I was still a loveable, worthy and kind person in asserting boundaries (in this case, only answering calls when I had the energy and space). But when we start to challenge an identity role we have played along with for some time, rather than acceptance for this 'new' version of ourselves, we often receive backlash. Anger and frustration are rife from loved ones. We're told, 'You've changed.' Because, well, we have. But not in the negative way that is suggested in these moments.

We train people how to behave with us. It really is that simple. If we are hyper available at all costs, then that is what is expected of us – to always answer the call, reply instantly to the text or be available in the DMs. If we never say no to anything, then of course others will expect that we are the yes gal. If we allow people to mistreat us – through their words or behaviours – without any level of standing up for ourselves, then it will continue.

The challenge here is that the good-girl complex can be so deeply ingrained in us that to live another way feels terrifying. We become convinced we are unlovable, even when asserting very simple, justifiable boundaries or a no that really should just seem commonplace.

Asserting boundaries

When I was a child, asserting boundaries with the adults in my life was near impossible. I would tread very carefully, not wanting to step a foot wrong, argue back or share the times I disagreed with certain beliefs or behaviours because that meant I would get into trouble and I wasn't being 'respectful'. I'd experience yelling, gaslighting or name-calling. None of that feels good, particularly to a young and impressionable girl, so it was much easier for me to just keep my mouth shut – to agree, even when every fibre of my soul was screaming, 'This is wrong! This isn't okay!' I trained myself to swallow my truth, my values and my worth. Because I was the 'good girl'.

There are still parts of the good girl in me that run rife. I haven't fully left her behind yet. And you know what, I probably never will. I value 'good' qualities in a person such as kindness, compassion and open-heartedness. For me, I recognise that things need to shift when playing the 'good girl' role comes at a cost to my own values and sense of alignment. But does that mean I shift gears straight into 'bad girl' territory? Absolutely not. This isn't about becoming the opposite of good. This is about redefining how you show up, labels aside. And *this* is where our boundaries come in.

When I first started to explore boundaries, I felt incredibly uncomfortable. I assumed that asserting boundaries meant I would be considered selfish, egotistical and perhaps even a bitch. These were all stories I had cultivated through years of having no boundaries. We see this playing out – especially with women – in the public eye, too. If she dare have an opposing view to the mainstream narrative, if she dare speak her mind, if she dare not smile because she's having a rough day, then she is labelled the troublemaker, the attention-seeker, the drama queen, the bitch. Not very nice labels to carry, are they? Good girl, nice girl and happy girl are much lighter labels to bear.

However, what I've come to learn in my own reclamation of boundaries is that you can still be kind, compassionate and loving, while teaching people the ways in which you wish to be treated. And in doing *this*, you actually allow yourself to give *more* kindness, love and compassion.

Anger's role in boundaries

This year, I booked a last-minute session with a kinesiologist to help me process some anger that had arisen after having conflict with a family member. I was proud of myself because I had finally asserted a boundary with them ('If you continue to speak to me in that way, do not contact me again'), however, rather than feeling lighter for it, I felt simmering rage. I was experiencing anger that I did not know how to move on my own. In this session, I was told that anger often arises when our boundaries have been crossed. My mind was blown. I repeat: anger arises when a boundary has been crossed.

I thought back to any time I have felt anger towards a friend or loved one in my life. And lo and behold, every moment the anger pointed to an overstepped boundary. The trouble with this was that – for the most part – I hadn't made my boundaries clear to the people in question. So while, yes, I was being mistreated in some ways, it actually wasn't on them. It was on me for not having asserted the boundary.

When it comes to relationships, I see anger as a gift because I know it points to a crossed boundary. And with *that* knowledge, we can start to assert our boundaries. But before we do this, it's important we identify the stories we're carrying with us that make us resistant to creating them in the first place. I feel this is often the missing link in creating boundaries that stick. Because we can only assert them, truly, when we feel confident and empowered in doing so. Let's walk before we run, shall we?

ACTIVITY: **The well-behaved complex**

Write down any stories you are telling yourself about what it means to be a 'good *insert identifying label here*'. Perhaps you can start to recognise where these stories have stemmed from and how they are, in fact, not even your own.

For example:

> The good girl in me tells me that I should say yes to every social catch-up that comes my way, even when I'm exhausted, can't be bothered or really just don't want to go along. I learned this behaviour from Mum, who always encouraged me to attend every party and social outing in my childhood. I never saw her say no to anyone. I now recognise that I can still be a kind-hearted person and lovingly decline outings or social catch-ups that do not align with my values.

Here is another example:

> The good girl in me replies to every message and answers every phone call, even when I have absolutely no energy or I don't want to engage with that person. I learned this behaviour in my corporate career, where hyper availability was rewarded and I was seen as a 'good' employee. I now recognise that I can still be exceptional at my job and give people my time on my own terms, without jumping every single time someone wants something from me.

Now it's your turn.

The good *label* in me says:

I learned this from:

I now recognise that:

Repeat this exercise for as many 'goody-goody' stories you are playing a role in. How many of these, truly, are serving you?

The importance of boundaries

In the past, when I thought about boundaries, I saw them as a giant STOP sign. Go straight to jail. Do not pass Go. Do not collect $200. My idea of boundaries didn't align particularly well with my idea of being a 'nice' person. I didn't want to block out people or appear unapproachable. What I know now is that there are loving, easy and kind ways to assert your boundaries in alignment with your values. And when you do *that*, the game changes.

Someone once shared a metaphor with me that your boundaries are like a key to your home. Having no boundaries is like throwing around your house keys willy-nilly. You, new follower on Instagram – you get a key! Hi, suss person down the street giving me the eye – you get a key! Yes, of course, reader, I'd love to give you one too! Here are keys for all!

What I love about this metaphor is that it blatantly illustrates firstly how ludicrous it is to allow every person you cross paths with in your life access to your home. (People, if you're not keeping up, we're not actually talking about your home – we're talking about *you*. *You* are the home in this instance. Your front door is the door to your energy and time.) It also illustrates how important your boundaries are in keeping you *safe*. Feelings of safety are incredibly important in asserting boundaries – our boundaries with our loved ones make it very clear what we will and won't accept for our own emotional, mental, physical and spiritual wellbeing. Is there anything more important than that?

ACTIVITY: **The keys to your home**

So, rather than throwing around your keys willy-nilly, have a think …
who will you allow the key to your front door? Truly?

_____

Who are the *key* people (pun intentional) in your life that you allow
access to all areas?

Next up, who will you invite over to your home – with the expectations
that they knock first? If you're not around, they can't let themselves in.
You're happy to share a cup of tea with them, but when it hits 4pm, they
have to leave (it's nap time, obviously).

From here, who will you allow into your front yard? Perhaps there's
dirty laundry on the dining table and you're not comfortable with these
people seeing your home in a mess, but they're welcome to sit with you
in the garden for a little while.

Now, who doesn't even need to know where your home is? They could
drive past the turn-off and have absolutely no idea you were there.

Re-evaluating your boundaries

When I first learned the concept in this exercise, I realised I was giving literal strangers the key to my front door. I was making tea for everyone – even with my home a mess, my trackies stained and my nap well overdue. Re-evaluating this was the start of a massive shift.

The people in my life who have access to all areas are a handful of my closest people – family members and some friends who have become family. I will drop everything for these people. They get access to me whenever they need. And I know the exchange will be mutual. They get a key, and I get one in return.

Those I allow into my 'home' have a little less access. When I have energy to spare, I'm absolutely available. When I don't, they might knock at my door and realise I am not home. This also goes for parameters I put in place when working with clients. For example, in a course I run, I have a very clear boundary that email contact is acceptable whereas personal DMs, texts or messages are not. I will not be available for those.

Then there are the people who might be invited to sit in my front yard every now and then. Maybe a new friend that I'm happy to take a beach walk with but likely won't spend hours on the phone with. Or perhaps my online community, where I may offer some guidance in the content I share or a free webinar, but will not offer direct guidance over Instagram DMs (because that sort of work is a professional boundary where I require payment in exchange for personal one-on-one time).

And finally, the strangers. Perhaps the people who think they know you, because you went to primary school together, but you could walk past them on the street and have no recollection of who they are. Or maybe that cousin's friend's cousin who your mum expects you to invite to your wedding to 'keep the peace'. You literally owe these people nothing. Harsh? Maybe. But it's the truth.

So, now that we are clear on the various boundary lines with the people in our lives, how do we *implement* them? What can boundaries look like?

Enforcing boundaries

One of the biggest boundaries I have ever enforced is playing out in my life right now. As I write this, I am 18 weeks' pregnant. My baby bump has popped, Trent and I call our little girl by her first name and I've even bought a pair of maternity jeans (I'm not really a jeans girl on the best of days, but it's a rite of passage I felt inclined to take part in).

Yesterday, at the chiropractor, while I was lying face-down on a maternity cushion (sweet relief), my chiropractor asked me, 'Have you made your pregnancy announcement yet?' I replied, 'Yes and no.' All of our loved ones – family, friends and those with VIP access to our front door – are very aware we are having a baby. In fact, not just those with VIP access (although they receive regular bump pics on request), but even those who are a little further removed. I live in a small town, so word of mouth is a real thing. That said, we haven't shared a social media announcement post and, before baby girl arrives, I'm not sure we will.

There are many reasons behind this decision that both Trent and I made together – long before baby even landed, might I add – however, one of the biggest reasons is prioritising our boundaries. For us, this is a time to be celebrated with our loved ones. It has been so beautiful to share real-life conversations, FaceTime calls to reveal the sex and just general life updates when crossing paths with people as we go about our lives. If someone isn't aware of the pregnancy by now, it's for a very real reason – we're likely not closely connected. For me, that sits well.

Now, this is obviously a case of each to their own. I *love* seeing my friends announce their exciting news online to the public. I am also fully aware that our decision to *not* share widely could cause some confusion or upset in others (but, in this instance, it's a case of damned if you do, damned if you don't. Pregnancy politics is a thing!).

Our decision to not share widely isn't about anybody else but us. Especially knowing that I have cultivated an incredible community of beautiful people invested in my life who would likely want to hear details of my pregnancy – specifics I'm not comfortable sharing right now – or even offer potentially very thoughtful but unsolicited advice in my DMs. I know how this works. It's part of the way I have chosen to show up and share my life online. It has served me very well, and has also offered much challenge. Any unsolicited advice, while well-meaning at the best of times, is just not something I am willing to open my energy to throughout this experience. I am a deeply intuitive person, and that side of myself – through my own self-awareness – becomes jeopardised with questioning my instincts and self-doubt when I hear about people's experiences. I have many people in my life I can turn to if I need to – I don't need to add any noise right now.

The irony in this is I know and love many a woman who finds the DM suggestions, and the mass excitement of strangers and loved ones alike, a very exciting, encouraging part of the pregnancy journey. To which I say, a-freaking-mazing! This is the thing to remember with our boundaries – they may not look the same on others as they do on us. Our boundaries are uniquely ours to own, despite what others may think or what they may trigger in others.

Two-way boundaries

It's just as much our responsibility to honour *other* people's boundaries, even if they differ from our own. So really, the act of boundaries goes two ways – honouring your own, and those of others. This is especially true in romantic relationships. Each of us has a very different operating system that is just as worthy of respect as our loved one's. And when we start to implement boundaries through clear communication in our relationships, the game can truly change.

Take, for example, my client Stacy (name has been changed). With a past of toxic exes, she noticed that there was a pattern playing out in her relationships where she would people please from the perspective of 'keeping the peace'. This people pleasing in a romantic context led to her putting her partner's needs before her own, which over time led to a build-up of resentment and passive aggression. Cue: little fights that really didn't need to happen.

Following some deep mindset work (the same that you have been working through in this book!), Stacy started to recognise that through clear communication of her own personal boundaries, and expressing her relationship needs while listening openly to her partner's as well, the entire relationship changed.

'Learning to put myself first by implementing and clearly communicating my boundaries – with my family, friends and especially with my partner – has made our relationship so much healthier!' she said. 'He's mentioned so many times how much happier I am, he loves the changes in me and we're reaping the rewards because of it!'

Implementing boundaries

To clarify your boundaries and work out how to start implementing them across your life, it's necessary to become super clear on what leaves you feeling aligned and energised versus what doesn't. From there, you can start to construct 'access points' to your energy.

Here are some of the ways I implement boundaries throughout my days:

- *Flight mode*
  Oomph. This little function is a game changer when it comes to accessibility, and one not to be taken for granted. My phone is on flight mode right now, and is constantly throughout the entire writing process. When I need to focus on a task at hand, the phone switches to flight mode. It's also an incredible function to use if you just need some quiet time – the calls, messages and check-ins can wait.

- *Not being hyper available*
  Right now, we are a collective energy that expects immediate access to and replies from messages, calls and DMs. Never before have we been more 'in contact', which, yes, has its benefits, however it can also add to energetic drain and serious fatigue if we are constantly in reaction-mode to the notifications, alarms and calls going off in day-to-day life.

  Especially in working for myself, I have noticed a huge volume of people calling for social catch-ups during my work hours. It's almost as if because I am self-employed, my time isn't considered as much as those who work nine-to-five.

Here are some of the ways I counteract my hyper availability:

- *Automated responses*
  I have an automated email response that goes out to every email in my inbox. I identified the key areas people were emailing to enquire about, which were to book a session with me, offer a brand partnership or gift, or ask a personal question. With this in mind,

my auto-response answers the commonly asked questions without me needing to reply directly each time. I also explain in my auto-response that my inbox is a quiet inbox and reply times can be expected within a week or so.

I'm grateful that, on a work front, I get to make the rules, but I understand this may not work for everybody, depending on your work capacity. However, this is also a really great way to manage your voicemail or even Instagram DMs. Remember, you train people in how to connect with you. If you are constantly replying immediately, then that is what will be expected. It doesn't make it 'right' or more impactful. People respect your boundaries when you make them clear. Just because you have received a text message, it doesn't mean you have to reply to it instantly. The same goes with phone calls – your time and energy matters. Return the call when you have the space to do so.

- *Closed inboxes*
  I used to have my Instagram Story responses open to everyone and my inbox would be constantly filled with reactions and comments (some deep, some simply 'Hahaha' because I'm super funny) and truly, this drained me. So, I turned my Story replies off. To take it further, I also added in my Instagram bio that I am not checking my DMs and for any enquiries, email is the best point of contact. Do people respect these boundaries? Not always. But at least I know, in my clarity of communication, that if people truly want access to my energy, they have been told the best way to contact me. I've made it very clear.

For you, this might mean muting the WhatsApp group that you really don't want to be alerted to every day or even uninstalling Facebook Messenger on your phone (game changer!). With so many access points demanding our energy and attention, streamlining to just one or two focal points of contact means you're less accessible, and also have far less to juggle when it comes to energy output versus input.

- *Screening calls*

  My friends and loved ones mostly know I dislike phone calls. It's a personal preference. I'm not someone who can just pick up a call on a Wednesday at 3pm and dive into an hour-long social catch-up. It drains me. No judgement if it's your jam, it just isn't mine. I far more appreciate a text check-in (with no expectation of reply times, because sometimes it takes me a few days) or even a scheduled FaceTime, like I do with one of my besties Em and her daughter every month. It's the first Thursday of every month and it's in the calendar. My energy is prepared – and excited – for it.

  I screen calls regularly – from loved ones, yes. I screen my mum's calls, my dad's calls, my sister's calls, my best friend's calls. They all know I do it, but as one of them said to me recently, 'I love when you answer, because I know I'm getting your full presence and you genuinely want to talk.' Exactly.

- *Mutual respect*

  I also love when I receive texts like I did this morning from close friends.

  The first read: 'Do you have the emotional bandwidth for a little rant?' Oomph. Music to my ears. This kind of check-in is so deeply respectful of one another's time and energy that no matter what I replied, I would feel appreciated and heard. In this instance, I said, 'Yep, I'll call you in ten, just heading out to cut laps of the property now!' (I'm implementing those flow-state feels!)

  The second text was from another friend right before I sat down to write this. It read: 'Can I give you a quick buzz by any chance? I'm feeling super stressed about …' I replied, 'I'm just about to jump into writing! Can I call you after?' She responded, 'No rush at all, whenever you are free and available.' Yes friends. This is mutual respect of boundaries, time and energy on both ends.

Compare these to a recent Instagram DM I received. This was during a particularly stressful time not only in my pregnancy, but we had also been at the emergency vet as our dog Archie had frightened us with two back-to-back seizures. It was terrifying and, suffice to say, deeply traumatic (thank the Universe for vets!). This DM was from someone who follows me on Instagram and has messaged me a handful of times. However, I do not personally know them and have never worked with them before. In the house analogy, they would be someone unaware of my 'address'. The message I received is something I call 'emotional dumping' – multiple paragraphs expressing a deeply traumatic experience this person had been faced with, their challenges throughout the recovery, and questions asking for my advice, guidance and, really, the things I offer in a paid 1:1 capacity in my mentoring calls.

When I received the message, I felt anger. Didn't this person realise how awful a time I was having? What made it feel okay for them to dump this trauma on me, without any warning, and expect a reply? (There wasn't even a 'I hope you're well …') Cue: crossed boundary. My anger quickly dissipated and was replaced with compassion. She was deeply struggling, that was clear. She felt safe to share with me, which was comforting in a way. Still, this was not my responsibility. Just a year ago, I would have replied as the fixer, helper, pleaser. But I knew, in this moment, it was time for me to – lovingly – assert some boundaries.

This was my reply: Hi angel, I so appreciate you reaching out to me and trusting me with your story. Unfortunately, I am at energetic capacity and have to prioritise my own wellbeing and that of my family and clients right now. With that in mind, I am unable to do your question any justice via an Instagram message. I hope you understand and I wish you nothing but the best on your journey. (*Insert red love heart*) To which she didn't respond. Siri, play Alanis Morissette's song 'Ironic'.

Honouring your boundaries

One of my past mentors with a massive community on social media explained to me that she could not possibly ever reply to every single message or email she received asking for guidance, help or just thanking her for her work. In fact, she would simply double-tap these messages (aka 'like' them) and move on. At the time, this was incredibly challenging for me to grasp. Those people had taken time out of their days to contact her. Didn't she owe them at least a little reply? I now realise that no, she does not. Just like no, I do not. Just like no, you do not.

Now, for you, maybe it isn't the stranger sliding into your DMs asking for guidance. But I can almost guarantee you have been on the receiving end of some form of 'emotional dumping'. The friend who only seems to contact you when they need a vent, perhaps? Or, like a beautiful client of mine, perhaps you're the family 'glue' holding everyone else together in a crisis. That could look like midnight phone calls holding loved ones in their distressed state while totally neglecting your own wellbeing.

Here is what I told my client in this exact situation recently: the more we can come to terms with not owing anyone anything, the more we can eradicate this mass societal expectation of the way people 'should' show up for us when we demand it of them – strangers, friends and family alike. These expectations blow my mind at times – that we are so quick to ask for something that could be simply googled or, dare I say it, paid for. And really, this behaviour will continue to be acceptable so long as we choose to accept it. I don't accept it anymore. This doesn't mean you need to be rude or unkind – as you can see in my reply on the previous page, it was heartfelt and honest but still was likely not what the receiver wanted to hear. But it's what I needed to say. *That* is the difference.

Here is another example. Yesterday, I received a DM from a beautiful former client, again, sharing paragraphs of an experience she has been navigating. I opened the DM, saw the volume of text and replied, 'Just acknowledging I have received but not read this message. I will read it when I have the space to do so. X' Now, I'm not sure when that time will be. (Need I remind you I am writing my first book while growing my first child?) My energy and time is limited. And no longer do I feel any guilt for asserting that or making it known. I'm not a bad person for choosing me in these moments. I'm a better person, because when I *do* show up, it's from the space of having energy to spare, rather than a martyrdom complex of 'everyone needing me'. And I know there will be seasons where I am more available – they've been in the past and will likely come again – but my boundaries right now are extra tight because my energy needs them to be. Remember, for you, this might not be a DM. It could be the multiple missed calls from aforementioned 'venting friend'. It could be a backlog of texts you just haven't gotten around to reading because your mental state needs a little introverted space right now. You are allowed that space. You are allowed that quiet time.

Let's start to put some of these boundaries in place.

ACTIVITY: **Boundaries**

Firstly, let's start with some easy ones. Think about where in your life you are currently *hyper available*. Where are you 'shoulding' versus 'wanting' with your time and energy for others? This could look like always answering phone calls, replying to messages right away or saying yes to catch-ups that drain you.

_____

Capture them all below:

Now, what are some really simple ways to start to lovingly enforce some personal boundaries? Use my examples earlier as inspiration, and list them below:

Now that you have some of the easier boundaries in place, it's time to get clear on the bigger ones. These are the ones that may require a tough conversation, or perhaps an instance where you may judge yourself for being 'rude', a 'bitch' or *insert outdated belief about setting boundaries here*. To start, think about any relationships in your life right now carrying a sense of obligation, anger or even resentment. Write down them, and the experience, below:

Now, with this in mind, how can you start to lovingly share your new boundaries with these people? I'll share some of my own recent examples to spark inspo.

Sharing new boundaries with love

I have always found it incredibly difficult to have challenging conversations with loved ones. I'm a peacekeeper at heart. Even when I *know* someone is being rude, critical or even abusive in their language or manner with me, people-pleasing Hollie used to cop it. I would swallow my hurt and put on a brave face. I mostly did this because I couldn't be bothered dealing with the repercussions if I stood up for myself, and I didn't want to exacerbate any tension. Also, I try my hardest to see everyone's perspective, even when it's at a cost to my own wellbeing. However, in the past year, something has shifted. Maybe it's good-girl fatigue or coming into my own more (thank you, Saturn return!), but I'm actually terribly drained by keeping quiet constantly. I am surrounded by wonderful people with beautiful hearts, so why would I choose to accept anything less than that?

Enforced boundary: example one

There is a history of abusive language and communication in my
family. I can see very clearly that this way of communicating stems
from family members' family members, so I have accepted the poor
behaviour in the past, given that I know deep down these people love
me, despite their words and behaviour. However, something shifted in
me recently that recognised I don't deserve this. Perhaps as a child and
even adolescent, it was more challenging for me to assert boundaries,
however now – as a grown woman about to start her own family –
I recognise that if I am allowing people to speak to me a certain way,
then that is on me. I'm accepting poor behaviour.

Now, the first few times I have asserted these new-found boundaries,
they were said with a quivering voice after many a pep talk from
aforementioned beautiful-hearted friends. It's *not* easy to enforce a new
way of behaviour after almost three decades of accepting a different way.
But while perhaps uncomfortable, and even fear-inducing, I have found it
truly is the only way to really start to back yourself.

This boundary – of teaching people how I wish to be spoken to –
has simply been as follows: 'If you continue to speak to me in this way,
I will be ending the conversation.' Plain and simple. That could relate
to yelling, name-calling or abusive language like swearing. The key
with this is that once you have stated this boundary, you must back it
up. If they *do* continue (which they likely will the first couple of times –
learned behaviour, and all that), then it is your opportunity to end the
conversation. To hang up mid-sentence. To screen the calls. To leave
the room. I have done this very assertion, and the calls have continued.
To which I have sent this message: 'I do not appreciate being yelled at,
and will not continue this conversation. If you plan to continue to be
abusive, please no longer contact me.'

Your boundary has been asserted – clear and simple. It is now up to the receiver to either respect it (what a win!) or neglect it. The latter basically enforces to you they care very little for your boundaries, meaning they care very little for *you*. This isn't on you – this is their stuff. But now you know you have communicated clearly, made your boundaries known and have a very real 'out' if the poor behaviour continues.

Perhaps for you, the boundary with loved ones isn't as intense as my above example. I enforced one with my dad just recently, which was a brilliant opportunity for me to practise what I preach in lovingly sharing when a boundary has been crossed. In this instance, Trent and I had just found out we were having a little girl. Being pregnant during a global pandemic meant that we shared this exciting news with our loved ones on FaceTime. I had asked my parents not to mention the sex to my siblings, as we were waiting to call them. So, you can imagine my frustration when the following day, I received a text from my brother congratulating me for the little girl we were having (thanks, Dad). Cue: anger. Hello, crossed boundary. I called Dad straight away and the conversation could not have been smoother or more well received. I simply explained my side, without any anger: 'Dad, I appreciate you are excited about our news, but I did ask you not to mention this to anyone, and I'm disappointed that now we don't have the opportunity to share this directly.' Dad couldn't have been more apologetic and understanding. In fact, although he can be quite stubborn, I received multiple calls and texts following this conversation, apologising for the crossed boundary and explaining that it all came from his excitement. I felt heard, and the anger dissipated. The weight was lifted. This is the power of an enforced boundary.

Enforced boundary: example two

Part and parcel of having a public profile is opening yourself up to criticism, backlash and, unfortunately, bullying behaviour from time to time. I have experienced countless trolls in my time of sharing my words and heart openly (love is like a target for trolls in a warped way – like moths to a flame). A recent example involved receiving public criticism from women known to me who, in the past, I would have considered friends, making it very clear that they disagreed with an aspect of my work and life. Now, I'm all for love beyond agreeance and constructive conversation, however, this specific experience felt incredibly painful to be on the receiving end of. I was given a nickname, there were clear lies being told to a public audience about an experience they had with me and it was the first instance in my life where I felt bullied. Add to the fact these were women I knew, and the shaming really took its toll on me mentally. I was not okay.

I didn't speak up in fear of adding 'fuel to the fire' and, truly, I just wanted the dust to settle. I was terrified of upsetting people – as it appeared I already had – and decided not to engage in conversation with those who clearly didn't wish the best for me or want to have a constructive conversation offline (read: not needed for the public eye). Six months went by, and I received a message from one of the women. In the message, she made it clear that she was unsure what had happened but she truly wished me no ill will and asked if we could please discuss the experience over the phone. At the time of receiving this message – six months after the fact – I no longer wanted to make amends. The dust had settled, as far as my energy was concerned. I'd come to terms with it, and didn't have anything to say. And that is precisely what I said in my reply. That I appreciated the message, that it was a challenging time for me and that, while I wished her well, I did not have the capacity for any conversation. Put simply, I chose not to have this connection anymore.

While potentially painful to the person on the receiving end, as I mentioned, I am surrounded by people who treat me with love and kindness, and would never treat me the way I had been treated in this instance. I didn't need to make amends, as I was surrounded by love. The only reason I would take that call would be to appease someone else – not me. Perhaps people-pleasing Hollie in the past would have said yes, let's sort this out – water under the bridge. But newfound Holz is a different breed. You can still be love and light *and* tell someone, 'No, that wasn't okay with me.' You can still be love and light *and* say, 'I do not have any energy or time for this.' You can still be love and light *and* say, 'I do not want to be your friend anymore.'

Now, there have likely been times when people you know and love have spoken to you, or treated you, in a way that has crossed a boundary of yours. Perhaps there is someone in your life who uses passive-aggressive communication, which leaves you questioning their intent. Or maybe you have a friend who is constantly putting you down under the guise of 'humour', which leaves you feeling second best. It needn't be straight-out public bullying or shaming to indicate a crossed boundary. Remember, more often than not, our anger will indicate to us where a boundary has been overstepped. Like a barbed-wire fence, it will prick right up. Rather than pulling the fence down to make room for the overstepping, how can you hold the barrier firmly, even when it may cause a little sting to the person in question?

Now is the time for you to highlight any difficult conversations that perhaps you are due to have right now. Write them all down below:

If you're not ready for these conversations in person, a brilliant technique is to write a letter to the person in question – where you release every emotion, word, feeling and tension point freely. They will never see this letter because it is about you, not them.

However, letter-writing release aside, know that should any poor behaviour continue, it's likely it will not stop until you assert yourself, and your boundaries, directly and clearly, and opt to no longer take part in a dynamic that is not serving your highest good. Because you're worthy of no less.

CHAPTER 9 **SUMMARY**

Your takeaways:

- Start to identify your 'good girl' behaviours, and recognise where they have been learned and how they may be hindering you or bringing you out of alignment.

- Complete the 'Keys to your home' exercise to identify clearly who has what level of access to your energy.

- Get clear on the people causing you any anger or resentment right now due to a crossed boundary. How can you enforce new boundaries? Do you need to have any difficult conversations?

- Write any releasing letters for those conversations you are not yet ready for.

Stretch target:

- Make use of flight mode, automated replies and phone screening to counteract your hyper availability. Start to engage only when you have the energy and desire to.

CHAPTER 10

Integration

As I write the final chapter of this book, my small town has entered a seven-day lockdown. This means we can only leave our homes for limited reasons – daily exercise, a grocery run or essential work.

This is actually quite fitting for me as I write this, as in this chapter, we are journeying into 'integration' territory. And often, integration can feel like a whole lot of nothing. After a solid journey deep into your mindset – reprogramming your brain, creating new habits, starting to shift into alignment and perhaps even setting some new boundaries (big deal!) – it will likely feel very uncomfortable to all of a sudden stop the 'doing'. To pull up stumps, cease and desist. And yet, that is exactly what I am going to ask you to do. (Cue discomfort!)

The integration process of *any* personal development lesson is often the missing link to embodying the shifts and changes you have worked so hard to create in your space. And the reason we skip this part is – as usual – it seems 'too simple'. If you're anything like me, it even becomes a little bit addictive to notice the growth and changes in you as a result of doing 'the work', and so, as you read this, you likely already have your next personal development book piled up in a very Instagrammable side-table stack, alongside a phone crammed with podcasts to dive deep into and maybe even a dog-eared journal ready to commence that next program you signed up to. How comfortable would you feel if I asked you to just put that all to the side for a moment? How comfortable are you in the space between? Can you take a rest stop?

Why we need integration

Reflect on the journey you have just embarked on. You've worn in your hiking boots (your daily foundational practices for living in alignment), you've been traversing some rough terrain with the help of your compass (values) and road map (path to alignment), and your water bottle is constantly on the refill (your new energetic practices). But even Edmund Hillary would tell you that to get anywhere worth going, you need to take breaks. You need space to rest, recalibrate and, in this instance, let the lessons land.

There was a stage in my life where I didn't take integration seriously enough. In a single year – one year alone – I had completed a ten-day silent meditation retreat (yes, I was terrified and no, I have no idea how I did it), sat in multiple ceremonial circles for the first time (from ceremonial cacao in Bondi to breathwork in Bali), undertook a tantric embodiment practice and even explored past-life regression, deep kinesiology practices and cord-cutting. Not to mention the multiple self-help books cramming my bookshelf, the daily meditation practice and strict regimens around all of my other spiritual practices. I even had 15 oracle decks. I was a woman on a mission. Each 'hit' of personal growth left me wanting more. And I didn't see an issue with it. There were worse things to be addicted to, right? But, like any addiction, it became a vice – an outlet – and an escape from actually sitting with my stuff. I needed to just be with myself and carve out the space and quiet to process the multitude of shifts I had created in my life.

The following year after my spiral into 'the work', I went in the exact opposite route. It's almost like I turned around and headed *back* the way I had come. I gave most of my oracle decks away. I took a break from meditation and journalling. I stopped offering intuitive readings, and even swapped out plant medicine for more illicit substances. I wanted to feel 'human' again – I had gone too far down a winding path that left me dazed and confused, with little tread left in my hiking boots. The foundations had worn away. My bottle was out of water. I'd lost my compass and map. So I stopped walking.

I don't want this for you. Let my all-or-nothing past thinking be your Sherpa at this part of your trek. Take a seat – you've earned it. You have done *such* an incredible job of journeying to this point. But to keep going? We need resilience, perseverance and a big, giant break. So, before we take a breather, it's time to take stock on how far we've come.

ACTIVITY: **Reflections**

Cast your mind back to the version of you when you first started reading this book. Who were you then? What were your biggest challenges? How did you feel about the road ahead? Jot it all down below.

Now, it's time to send yourself some gratitude for the journey you have been on. Whether you feel exhausted by the hike or you know you have a big journey ahead, write down all of the ways you have shown up for yourself over the course of this book.

Perhaps some prompts to consider are:

- My new foundational practices for living in alignment are …

- My key values to live by are …

- I maintain my energy each day by …

- I connect with my intuition each day by …

- The limiting beliefs I have reframed so far include …

- The new stories I tell myself are …

- The friendships I am excited to nurture more are …

- I will nurture my friendships by …

- Boundaries I am ready to assert include …

What you have just captured above is a hell of a journey. Can you see how much you have shifted in such a short amount of time? This is where I am going to remind you of your vowels. Yes. Just briefly, we're casting our mind back to kindergarten (oh my gosh, you're so cute!).

Repeat after me: 'A, E, I, O, U.'

A – Awareness and Action

E – Embodiment

I – Integration

O – Ownership

U – Understanding

Awareness and Action

You've nailed this part. Remember, you can't possibly un-know what you know. You've walked the path, learned the lessons and (hopefully) completed the activities. Awareness and action go hand in hand – it's not enough to know the path you're taking if you decide to never walk it. The same goes with living aligned to your values and, ultimately, putting yourself first as a result. It's not enough to do the work on the 'knowing' – we always have to back it up with the 'doing'. *That* is where real change happens. And that has been your entire journey already in reading this book.

Embodiment

I see embodiment as actually walking your talk. Because you can quote this book until you're blue in the face (please don't do that), you can share all of the pages on your Insta stories (please, *do* that) and purchase it as a gift for all of your friends (you're the best, thank you!), but unless you are actually embodying these lessons, what's the point? This is why the space between the knowing, the doing and the embodying is *key*. Because this is the space where the lessons actually land. Where you *become* what you know, and how you show up. This, my friends, is *true* alignment – in the *being*.

Integration

Here we are – the integration process. Now, integration isn't so much about putting the books down, turning off the poddies and throwing all of your practices away. Heck no! Integration is not stopping entirely (like 'all-or-nothing me' two years ago would have believed). Integration is just about taking a breather between journeys. Your integration process will be deeply personal. Perhaps it's taking a week or two to start putting your notes into practice – playing with what feels good and what doesn't. Maybe integration for you is doing something super-duper 'human', such as cocktails with your aligned friends or buying a beautiful piece of jewellery to remind you of the journey you've just been on. What integration *isn't* is rushing out to do the next course, buy the next book or even re-read over these notes again. Put the book down (once you've finished, we're almost there!). What does a break look like for you?

ACTIVITY: **Integration**

Finish this sentence: I will take a break from doing any personal development work by …

There you have it. Go and do that.

Ownership

Now, ownership is a key component to integration. That is, personal ownership of how *you* show up in embodiment and alignment as regular practices. You don't need me to hold your hand on the path anymore – even in the really rocky bits – you've got this! But it does take a lot of mental pep talking at times. Remember our favourite of the inner voices, self-belief? This is where we invite her in to stay. How can you take ownership of the work you have done so it doesn't just sit pretty on your bookshelf collecting dust? How can you continue to show up in the practices so that your life is a reflection of these lessons?

ACTIVITY: **Pep talk**

Invite forward the voice of self-belief and imagine you are handing her a microphone. What does she have to say to you about staying true to the lessons and the journey you've just been on? How will you continue to take ownership to show up in alignment and put yourself first?

Now, allow self-doubt to grab the mic – just for a moment – and capture below any niggling doubts or even excuses for why you may not stick to these practices:

Beautiful. Now, pass that mic over to self-worth – what does she have to say to you?

Finally, does self-belief have any final words for you?

Remember, with any of these beliefs that feel particularly sticky or challenging to move through, you've got your trusty Five Whys practice to turn to. Use it as often as you need to continue coming back to your truth.

Understanding

After we learn something new that has changed us or our lives
(bold statement, but I'm hoping at least some of you feel this way now),
often we want to shout it from the rooftops! Sing it to the crowds! Jump
up and down on Oprah's couch like a mad person! While very exciting
and, yes, filled with beautiful intention (we just want everyone to feel as
good as we do, right?!), what can actually happen is a reverse effect to
our initial intention – we start 'should-ing' on other people: 'You really
should read this book; it will help you!' 'You should consider what your
values are and how you're caring for your energy.' 'You should practise
your Five Whys – here, I'll show you!' And this can start to disconnect
others from their own wants.

Remember, just because we choose to live a certain way, it doesn't
mean it's the way our family, friends or lovers want to live too. And
when we start should-ing all over them, well, there really is no good
that comes from it. But you already know that, right? You are walking
your path. They are walking theirs. And sometimes, the paths may
cross and you can walk arm in arm together. But also, lots of the time,
you will be happily strolling yours, right beside them, and not need the
paths to cross over. This doesn't make either of your paths the 'wrong'
one. Just different. We like different. We want different. It's what makes
life interesting.

This is where understanding is so key. Understanding that while you
are on your own journey, so are your loved ones. And even with the
best intentions, we truly do not know what is best for them. They have
to figure it out themselves. Maybe you'll have someone ask you, 'Hey,
you seem different. What's changed?' which is a beautiful invitation
to share more about what you're working through. But remember, not
everyone is going to be interested. Some people are wearing different
hiking boots. Some people's paths are a little windier so they need more
breaks. There is nothing wrong with different. Let it be.

Your takeaways:

- Establish how you will take a break from personal development work. What will that look like for you?

- Create space between completing this part of your personal development journey and whatever comes next.

- It's time to give yourself a little pep talk! How will you continue to show up in your life embodying the lessons you have learned on this journey? And how will you hold yourself to account?

Stretch target:

- Revisit your Five Whys exercise any time your self-talk wavers during integration.

Conclusion

So, there you have it – you're officially no longer a people pleaser! From this day forth, you will be living with aligned magnetism, attracting only great things, enforcing boundaries that are tough but loving and embodying an unwavering mindset.

Just kidding.

It's probably a good way to wrap things up by sharing with you that I *still* identify as a people pleaser some of the time. Nowhere near as much as I used to – thankfully – but yes, I still do. As Richard Bach's saying goes: 'We best teach what we most need to learn.' In writing this book, I have literally been completing the activities as I go. Some of them – especially the boundaries pieces – have left me feeling super uncomfortable. I'm putting off three challenging conversations with loved ones right now because I'd still rather avoid the discomfort of potential conflict. So please, go gently with yourself. This is not an overnight 'fix'.

Just because you've read a book on people pleasing, doesn't make you an expert on no longer ever people pleasing. Heck, I wrote the book and I'm no expert. There's a very nice humanness in admitting we don't have it all figured out – and you know what? I don't think we will ever have everything figured out. But what we *will* have figured out are the practices, methods and levels of self-awareness that allow us to create empowered change in our lives. Some days, that is going to be super-duper easy for you. Other days (or weeks, or months), it will be the last thing you want to do. Need I remind you of my favourite saying from our main man, Dr Phil? 'Life is a marathon, not a sprint.'

Go gently. I'll be walking my path right beside you.

Acknowledgements

The birth of this book, while a lifetime in the works, is deeply interconnected with the birth of my little girl. I received this book deal in my first trimester, wrote the entire book in my second trimester and it launches the same week we celebrate her first birthday!

With that in mind, I'd like to acknowledge the key people who truly went above and beyond during a stage of my life that was enormously pivotal, challenging and also incredibly rewarding.

To my family – Mum, Dad, Tyler and Carmen – I know that no matter what we are moving through individually you always have my back, and that means more to me than anything else. Thank you, Mum and Dad, for always encouraging me to pursue a life path that makes me happy. This book is here because of that.

To the friends who really stepped in when I wasn't able to give much back, I will forever look back on this time in my life with the deepest gratitude in my heart for the ways you went above and beyond for me, Trent and our little girl. Special thanks to Leah Pitman, Emily Steven, Jessica Lear, Jessica Maher, Nikki Gonda, Brittany Eastman, Stevie Nupier, Taylor Winterstein, Kate Holm, Cassey Maynard, Janoah Van Kekem, Monica Pacheco, Blake Worrall Thompson, Shani Timms and, of course, my sis, my gal, my love, my world: Carmen Azzopardi. I love you all so much.

To my friends who have become family up here on the Northern Rivers, for holding us through pregnancy, birth, floods and beyond – thank you for stepping in as family when we really needed it. Thank you, Mum, for the constant visits up and help around the home in the times you could.

To my right-hand woman, Jessica Silsby – I genuinely do not know where my business or vision would be without you. Thank you for being as committed to this work as you are and making it fun!

To Ludmilla Oliveira – I will never forget the day we crafted my vision together, and only a few short months later landed this deal. Thank you for believing in me.

To my publisher, Kelly Doust – we finally got to create magic together after meeting all those years ago. Thank you for believing in me as a writer and helping make one of my greatest dreams come true! I will be forever grateful. Thank you to Jordanna Levin for introducing and championing me, my words and my work to Kelly all those years ago.

This book would not be what you see today without the multitude of wonderful people who helped behind the scenes to put it together. Thank you to my editor, Ally McManus, for your beautiful additions to my words, and to designer Emily Thiang for the on-point creative work that truly captures my essence. Thank you to Kevin, Keiran, Elizabeth, Rosie and the entire Affirm Press team for supporting and backing a new writer on the scene like me.

To the beautiful Manifestation and Magic Intake Six women – thank you for being my crash testers for all of the concepts and meditations in this book. I also wouldn't have been able to write this book without the experience of mentoring and guiding so many wonderful clients in both group and one-on-one sessions over the years – thank you to those of you who have trusted me in some way with your journey.

My beautiful online community that has followed my journey from the very beginning – I hope this book has been worth the wait. Thank you for your constant celebration of my life and work – it doesn't go unnoticed. Thank you to those of you new to my work and my world through this book – it means a lot to have you here.

Beautiful Zoe Bosco, where do I begin? Our birth doula turned fourth member of our family. I couldn't have done any of this without you. Thank you for being a channel of endless wisdom and for offering your gifts so freely throughout the process of birthing both my book and my daughter. It is an honour to be doing life by your side, Zo. I love you dearly.

Trent, to know you is to love you and I think everyone in your life can attest to that. You are the love of my life, my rock and soul mate, and I couldn't do any of 'this' – being all of the work I do in the world – without you. You are my strength and my greatest supporter, and you have believed in me from the very beginning. I simply would not be the woman I am today without you. Little girl and I are so blessed to have you. I love you with all of my heart.

Thanks to my fur babies, Lola-Lou and Archie-Rose, for keeping me company as I wrote (and being my first children, obviously).

And the best last, my little girl. Sweet little Fire Petal. My muse. So much of what I learned and wrote in this book was thanks to the fire you ignited in me from the moment you were conceived. You are a force, my girl. I dedicate these teachings, these words and my entire life legacy to you. Thank you for choosing me. I will love you forever. x